Neuromarketing
The Value of Price.
Psychological Keys for Setting Successful Prices

JIMMY FAJARDO

Content

Chapter 1: Price Doesn't Exist in Reality

All prices are a mental construct. No product is worth what it costs to make it.

Note to the reader: This chapter has a single mission: to make you see something you've been looking at your whole life without truly understanding. After reading it, you'll never write a number on your product label or in your e-commerce listing the same way again.

The night everything changed

You close your laptop at 11:47 at night.

You've spent the last two hours browsing sales platforms, comparing your catalog to the first-page results. You've opened twelve different competitor tabs. You've reviewed your production costs, your printing or manufacturing margins, and shipping rates. And after all that exhausting analysis, you arrive at the same frustrating conclusion as always:

I don't know what price to sell this for.

It's not because you don't know how to do math. It's not because you're unfamiliar with your niche. It's because you feel there's a hidden truth somewhere—a correct number, a fair price, a mathematical figure that the market has determined to be appropriate for your product—and you simply can't find it.

That night, without realizing it, you were chasing a ghost. You were looking for something that doesn't exist.

The great misunderstanding about the value of a product

There is a silent belief that most creators, authors, and online marketers carry with them from the first day they tried to launch a product to market:

There is a right price. And my job is to calculate it.

It's such a natural premise that almost no one questions it. But it's a deadly trap for your profits and royalties.

- **It doesn't exist.**the right price.
- **It doesn't exist.**the fair price.
- **It doesn't exist.**the target price.

What exists is the perception of price. And that perception lives solely and exclusively in the mind of the person who clicks the "Buy" button.

This isn't cheap philosophy. It's pure neuroscience. It's cognitive psychology applied to consumer behavior. Understanding this is a game-changer for your business.

A Tale of Two Cafes (Context is Everything)

Let's do a thought experiment. Imagine two cups of coffee. Identical. Same origin, same beans, same temperature, same volume. An expert barista couldn't tell them apart blindfolded.

- **Cup A (Neighborhood Cafe):**A plastic table, paper napkins, a television playing the news. The price on the board: $3,500 pesos.
- **Cup B (Specialty Coffee):**Warm lighting, premium packaging, the barista explains the altitude at which the coffee was grown. The price on the artisanal menu: $18,000 pesos.

Same grains. Price five times higher. So what is the "right" price for the physical product?

The question has no answer because it's poorly phrased. The price isn't in the dark liquid. It never was. The price lies in the experience the customer anticipates, in the packaging design, in the story your metadata tells, and in how the buyer feels upon purchasing it.

You are not selling a physical object or a digital file. You're selling what that product means at that exact moment. And this rule applies equally to a book, a technical tool, or a consumer item.

What neuroscience says (The wine experiment)

In 2008, a team of researchers published a study that shook the foundations of marketing. They placed several participants in a functional magnetic resonance imaging (fMRI) scanner and gave them wine to taste. It was exactly the same wine, served from the same bottle.

But they altered a small detail on the product label:

- Half of the participants were told that the bottle cost $10.
- The other half were told it cost $90.

What happened in their brains?

People who believed they were drinking the $90 wine showed significantly greater activation in the medial orbitofrontal cortex, the brain region associated with pleasure and reward. They didn't just say it tasted better. Their brains literally experienced more physical pleasure.

The product was identical. The price tag was different. The brain processed two completely different realities. This is known as price as a signal of quality. And it has a direct implication for your store:

When you sell cheaply, you don't just earn less money. You're delivering a neurologically inferior experience to your customer, even if the actual quality of your product is impeccable.

The price you see and the price you feel

Your brain doesn't process prices rationally. When a customer sees the price on your product page, three simultaneous reactions occur in less than two seconds:

1. **The Pain of Paying (Insula Activation):**This brain region is associated with physical pain. It activates when we see a high price. Paying activates the same neural network as suffering a blow. Neuroscientists call it "the pain of paying."
2. **The Search for the Anchor:**The brain needs context. High compared to what? If you don't have a good cover design, high-quality images, or optimized descriptions to position your product as superior, the customer's brain will use the cheapest Chinese product it finds on the platform as an anchor.
3. **The Limbic Assessment:**The emotional brain processes the story behind the product before analyzing the price. The box design, the visible reviews, the quality of the cover image... all of that is evaluated before the number.

So, where does the price really lie?

If the price doesn't come from adding up your manufacturing costs plus a profit margin, where does it come from?

The price lies in the perceived distance between the customer's desire/pain and the clarity of your solution.

The more intense the desire or the problem, the higher the price the customer will readily pay. Consider this across different product niches:

- **Example 1 (Specialized Sports):**A weekend angler won't pay a fortune for fishing bait. But a competitive fisherman competing in a tournament won't question the price of imported tackle or a premium fermented bait mix if his goal is to land a heavy cachama. The problem (losing the trophy) is enormous. The solution (the right product) is priceless.
- **Example 2 (Publications):**A generic board game book competes for pennies in the store. But a manual that breaks down proven mathematical systems for mastering roulette or poker isn't perceived as just a "paper book"; it's seen as an investment that generates a return.

- **Example 3 (Children):** An ordinary children's book is just printed paper. But a series of magical illustrated stories that guarantee a parent can help their child fall asleep peacefully and without screens solves a major family problem. The perceived value multiplies.

Your price doesn't depend on the cost of production. It depends on how much the problem you solve hurts or how much pleasure you guarantee.

The strategic mistake of looking to the sides

Let's return to the midnight scene, in front of the screen. What you were doing is called market-referenced pricing. It's the most common mistake in e-commerce and self-publishing.

When you use the prices of your competitors' products on the first page of search results as a benchmark for setting your own price, you're implicitly accepting that your product is identical to theirs. That you're a commodity. And when you match everyone else's prices, the only variable you leave the customer to use in their decision is to find the cheapest option.

You enter a war of attrition (especially in international markets where others can absorb lower margins) in which only the one with the lowest costs survives. You don't want to play that game.

Price is a message, not a label.

To dominate the market, you need to install a new mindset in your trading strategy. From today onward, price is no longer just a simple mathematical result on your dashboard.

Price is your first marketing argument.

When you put a number in front of your customer, you're projecting your brand's DNA. You're silently telling them:

- *This is the level of quality of the materials/content I offer.*
- *This is the transformation I guarantee.*
- *This is the kind of discerning buyer who deserves to take this home.*

A low price not only reduces your royalties or profits, it also conveys questionable quality. Conversely, a premium price, supported by a consistent visual presentation and SEO that captures the exact search intent, activates a high-end expectation in your customer's mind even before they open the package.

Chapter 2: How the Brain Processes Numbers on the Screen

Basic neuroscience of pricing: amygdala, prefrontal cortex and the pain of payment in product trading.

Inside your customer's brain, a millisecond battle rages every time they see your product's price. One part of their brain wants to add it to their cart, while another screams for them to close the tab. Your job—as a salesperson, author, or creator—is to know which part is winning and how to tip the scales through your listing, packaging, and positioning before they even look at the price.

The scene that repeats itself with every click

The buyer lands on your product page, whether it's on your online store or on a massive platform.

Their eyes go straight to the number. They always go straight to the number. Before reading the description bullets, before checking the rich content (A+), before processing a single line of the technical specifications.

At that moment—that precise moment when his eyes find the number next to the buy button—something happens that he doesn't control, that you can't see, and yet it almost completely determines whether that cart will end up paid for or abandoned. His brain is processing the price.

And it's not doing it in the rational way you imagine.

The brain doesn't read numbers. It feels them.

There's a very convenient illusion in e-commerce: we believe that when a shopper sees the price of an item, they analyze it. They logically compare it with other browser tabs. They assess whether the materials or the number of pages justify the cost and coldly decide if it's worth it.

It's a nice illusion, but neuroscience shows it's false. The reality is more interesting (and more useful for optimizing your conversion): The brain senses the price before it thinks about it.

The actual sequence is not see → analyze → decide.

The actual sequence is see → feel → justify.

If the decision "this is too expensive" has already been made on an emotional level, your product's technical description won't convince anyone. It will only give permission to a mind that has already decided to leave the page. To understand why, you need to understand three "characters" that operate within your buyer's mind.

The three actors in the neurological drama

When a user evaluates your product, there are three brain systems cascading into action, each with its own agenda and speed.

Actor 1: The Amygdala (The Budget Guardian)

The amygdala is the oldest brain structure. Its original function is to detect threats and generate an immediate alarm. A predator in the dark. A fleeting shadow.

For the modern amygdala, a price perceived as "high" relative to the product's initial visual impression triggers the exact same mechanism as a perceived threat. It generates a micro-response of alertness. Subtle tension. The first seed of rejection. All of this occurs in approximately 120 milliseconds, before the customer has even finished mentally processing the figure.

Actor 2: The Anterior Insula (The Financial Pain Sensor)

If the amygdala is the security guard, the anterior insula is the sensor of emotional pain.

This region processes unpleasant experiences, and various studies (such as those by researcher Brian Knutson at Stanford) document that the act of paying activates the same brain region as physical pain.

When your customer sees the total cost (especially if there are hidden shipping fees), their brain instantly assesses whether parting with that money is going to "hurt." If the price exceeds what they visually expected, a signal of discomfort travels through the system before logic even kicks in. This explains why someone might desperately want your product and still close the page feeling that "it's too much money."

Actor 3: The Prefrontal Cortex (The Late Rationalizer)

This is where conscious thought resides. The kind that compares features, reads reviews, and justifies the purchase.

But it has a serious problem: It arrives late.

By the time the prefrontal cortex starts processing the benefits of your product, the amygdala has already sounded the alarm and the insula has already registered the pain. What the prefrontal cortex does in most purchases is not to decide, but to rationalize what the emotional system has already felt.

*"It's very expensive"*It's not the result of auditing your manufacturing costs; it's the verbal translation of an emotional pang.

The buying cascade: Two seconds that decide everything

This is what the neurological map looks like from the moment the product page finishes loading:

Time	Cerebral Region	What happens internally in e-commerce	The Hidden Verdict
0 – 120 ms	Amygdala	Threat detection. Does the product image look cheap but the price is high?	Safe vs. Suspicious
120 – 300 ms	Anterior insula	Pain assessment. How much will it "hurt" to add this to your cart?	Tolerable vs. Intolerable
300 – 800 ms	Limbic System	Emotional processing. What does the brand, cover, or packaging make me feel?	Desire vs. Indifference
800 ms – 2 s	Prefrontal Cortex	Rationalization. Reading of comic strips, reviews, and descriptions.	Justification of the emotion
After 2 seconds	Action	Click on "Add to Cart" or close the window.	Echo of the internal decision

The pain of paying is malleable

The pain of paying is not a fixed factor. The greater the gap between the price and the perceived value, the brighter the insula becomes. The more it hurts.

But the exact same price can trigger completely different levels of pain depending on:

- The quality of the images (Do they have cinematic lighting? Are there 3D mockups?).
- The story and copywriting of the listing.
- Social proof (reviews from other buyers).

The pain isn't embedded in the price tag. It's in the visual interpretation of the product. And that interpretation is easily influenced.

The story of the two children's books

To illustrate, imagine a parent looking for a gift and finding two sets of illustrated children's books at a large retail store. Both physical books cost exactly $18.99.

- **Book A:**It has a generic cover that looks like it was made with free templates. There's no rich content on the page; the description is a single paragraph of plain text, and there are no photos of the interior.
- **Book B ("Magic Tales"):**The cover features detailed illustrations and cinematic lighting. Scrolling through, the buyer sees beautiful graphics from inside, text explaining how these stories help children relax before bed, and reviews from relieved parents.

Same format. Same list price. In which of the two does the buyer's insula suffer more when swiping the card?

The answer is obvious. Book B reduced the pain of paying for it not by offering discounts, but by drastically increasing the perceived value through visual presentation and content. The price didn't change. The buyer's brain did.

What activates and what deactivates the system in product sales

To make this actionable in your catalog or sales listings, here's the neurological control panel:

What triggers the alarm (Amygdala/Insula):

- **Low quality images:**A pixelated photo of your product accompanied by a premium price is a neurological short circuit.
- **Surprise shipping costs:**The product costs $20, but at the last step of the checkout process, an unannounced $15 shipping fee appears. The island explodes, and the cart is abandoned.
- **Descriptive descriptions instead of transformative ones:**Saying "200-page book" instead of "the exact system that will make your next poker game profitable."
- **Lack of social proof:**Being the first to buy something without reviews activates the survival instinct (risk).

What turns off the alarm and reduces pain:

- **Focus on ROI or Transformation:**If you sell a high-cost, specialized fishing lure, the customer isn't buying sourdough; they're buying the guarantee of catching a large fish and winning the weekend tournament. The pain of paying disappears in the face of the promised glory.
- **Impeccable design and visual professionalism:**Packaging perceived as luxurious or a fast-loading website immediately soothes the amygdala.
- **Specific reviews:**Photos of customers using the actual product. Seeing that the "tribe" survived the purchase reduces the sense of risk.

The salesman who forgot he also has a tonsil

Almost no one talks about this: You, as a salesperson and creator, also have an amygdala.

You launch a new product. Three days go by and sales are slow. Your brain anticipates failure and rejection. Panic kicks in and you do something that destroys your brand positioning: you log into the control panel and drastically lower the price, or you put a "50% off" sticker all over the store.

Nobody asked you to. The market didn't reject your price; it simply didn't have enough traffic yet, or your keywords (the right long-tail keywords) needed SEO optimization. But your amygdala went into preemptive panic, and you implemented the price cut.

The buyer who arrives the next day reads this instantly: This product is perpetually discounted. It's not a high-quality item; it's clearance merchandise.

The insight that changes your listings

The price a customer accepts or rejects isn't the mathematical figure. It's the visual neurological experience that number triggers in their brain when compared to images of your product.

Your sales job isn't about setting the lowest possible price to compete with international manufacturers. It's about preparing the neurological ground. A price that lands on an optimized product page, with social proof and impeccable presentation, converts visits into sales. A price that lands on a neglected page dies before the customer even reads the first benefit.

The price battle is won in the design of your listing.

Chapter 3: The Exact Moment When the Buyer Decides

The first 3 seconds of price exposure and what triggers them on your product page.

There's a precise three-second window after a customer lands on your product page or clicks on your listing where the brain makes a decision that almost never changes. Once you understand the anatomy of this microscopic window, you can design your covers, images, and metadata so that the human decision-making algorithm always works in your favor.

Three Seconds on Screen

It's not five minutes reading reviews.

It's not an hour comparing technical specifications.

It's not an in-depth analysis of your book's index or your article's ingredient list.

Three seconds. That's the exact amount of time your product has to survive or die in the mind of the person who just clicked on your link.

What happens next—scrolling down, reading the comics, checking other users' opinions—is almost always the consequence of an instinctive decision that's already been made. The rest is the rational mind looking for excuses to confirm what instinct has already dictated.

Understanding what happens in those three seconds is like mapping the territory where conversion is won or lost in e-commerce.

The experiment that changed everything

In 2006, psychologist Ap Dijksterhuis of the University of Amsterdam published a study that shook the marketing world. His question was simple: When do people make better decisions, when they think long and hard or when they decide quickly and intuitively?

The results showed that for decisions with multiple variables (such as choosing a product from dozens of options on a results page), people who decided intuitively ended up more satisfied.

The neurological reason? Your subconscious brain processes up to 11 million bits of information per second. Your conscious brain processes barely 50 bits per second. When you present a user with a confusing list and ask them to "analyze" whether your price is fair, you're inviting the slower, less efficient system to take over. The fast, powerful system already made the visual decision upon seeing your first image. And it did so in three seconds.

Autopsy of a decision in E-Commerce: Second by Second

We're going to get inside your buyer's head in real time, right when the web page finishes loading and the "Buy Box" appears on the screen.

Second 1: Threat Assessment (Unconscious)

As soon as the eyes register the main image and the price figure, the amygdala asks a single question: Is this safe?

The brain instantly compares what it sees against three factors:

- **The internal anchor:**How much did the products next to yours cost on the search page?
- **The visual identity signal:**Does the image quality, the cinematic lighting of your cover, or the packaging justify this issue, or does it look like an improvised design?

- **Anticipatory pain:** An instant simulation of what it will feel like to part with that money.

Second 2: The Search for Permission (Preconscious)

If the main image and price didn't trigger an alarm of "this is a scam or poor quality," the prefrontal cortex kicks in: Can I justify this purchase?

The brain doesn't seek the truth; it seeks permission. It will scan your listing for keywords that confirm its biases. If the first second was positive, it will search your description for the exact benefits it wants to say yes. If the first second generated distrust, any small detail will serve as an excuse to leave the page.

Second 3: Crystallization (Implicit Decision)

The brain reaches a hardened conclusion. At this point, the user's finger is already moving toward the "Add to Cart" or "Back" button. Trying to reverse a negative decision at this stage with a wall of boring text in the description is futile.

The 4 Forces That Dominate the Screen

If three seconds is the battlefield, you must control the forces at work in your product listing.

Critical Factor	How to ruin your sale	How to use it to your advantage
1. The Search Anchor	Your product appears next to Chinese options for $2 and your thumbnail looks exactly	Your thumbnail makes a radical difference in the results. If you sell a roulette or poker system, your cover image projects financial authority and

Critical Factor	How to ruin your sale	How to use it to your advantage
	the same as theirs, but you charge $20.	exclusivity compared to generic, low-cost guides.
2. Visual Coherence	The product is premium, but there is a spelling mistake in the title (e.g., "Pele" instead of "Pelle" in a foreign market) that destroys confidence in the second one.	Perfect alignment. Images with flawless 3D renders, precise metadata, and a listing that exudes technical perfection and editorial quality.
3. The Magnitude of Desire	You're selling a generic children's book, highlighting that it has "good quality paper." Desire is low.	You sell "Magic Tales" optimized with copywriting that promises parents will help their children fall asleep quickly. The desire is enormous.
4. Digital Friction	Boring technical descriptions, vague promises, or doubts about whether the product will work for the customer's specific case.	Assertive listings. If you sell bait or a specialized recipe for catching large species (like cachama), the text guarantees that specific result without hesitation.

The most costly mistake in online commerce

There is a habit that destroys conversions of physical and digital products with devastating accuracy: presenting a premium price with amateurish packaging.

This happens when you launch a product and let the platform automatically assign thumbnails. Or when you write descriptions without keyword optimization and without formatting. In these cases, the price reaches a mind without an anchor of authority, without a properly defined problem, and without visual consistency.

A price presented on a poorly designed digital canvas is a price rejected before it is even evaluated.

The Conversion Framework: The sequence for your listings

To ensure the three-second window works in your favor and the algorithm rewards you with more visibility, you should structure your product page experience like this:

1. **Gain clicks with the Visual Anchor:**Before a customer sees your price on the product page, they must have clicked on your thumbnail among dozens of results. That thumbnail (your book cover, the main photo of your article) must convey such high perceived value that, by the time they reach your page, the customer already expects a higher price.
2. **Impact in the First Second (A+ Images):**Secondary photos or enhanced content should immediately justify the price. If it's a physical item, show its real-world use. If it's a book, showcase impeccable interior layouts.
3. **Describe the wound in the Title and Subtitle:**Don't sell features, sell the end result. The title should capture your buyer's exact search intent and promise to solve their problem.
4. **Zero Insecurities (Social Proof):**Make sure the best reviews or testimonials are easily visible. The brain needs to know

that others have already bought, tested, and survived to tell the tale.

If you design your digital presence respecting these first three seconds, price will cease to be a mathematical barrier and will simply become the last logical step for the buyer to get what they have already decided they want.

Chapter 4: Why Selling Cheap Destroys Your Brand and Drives Buyers Away

Low prices as a warning sign and the volume trap in digital trading.

There's a silent belief that destroys more catalogs, online stores, and self-publishing businesses than any algorithm change. It's the false premise that "selling cheap is a surefire way to gain volume." Here, you'll see, with neuroscience and basic math, why low prices don't attract committed buyers—they repel them. And why raising your prices is the smartest positioning decision you'll make this year.

The logic that seems perfect (and why it's sinking your store)

The line of reasoning of a creator or seller competing on price in international platforms is so clear that it's almost beyond question. It looks like this:

1. *If I price my product lower than my competitor's, more people will buy it.*
2. *If more people buy it, I'll climb in the store rankings.*
3. *If I climb in the rankings, I'll have massive sales.*
4. *If I have massive sales, my business will be a resounding success.*

Impeccable. Logical. Reasonable. And profoundly wrong.

Not because mathematics fails in an ideal world, but because it's based on a false premise about how the buyer's brain works: assuming that the consumer always prefers the cheapest option. The reality, uncomfortable but liberating, is exactly the opposite.

What the price tag screams in the search results

Imagine a user is searching for a specialized solution. For example, an advanced manual with mathematical strategies for mastering roulette or poker, or perhaps a specific fermented formula for sport fishing for large species. The search results show three options with similar covers:

- **Product A:**It costs $2.99.
- **Product B:**It costs $14.99.
- **Product C:**It costs $35.00.

Which one do you click on first?

If the buyer is genuinely investing time in solving their problem (winning at the casino or securing their fishing trophy), their survival instinct doesn't lead them to the cheapest option. It leads them to the middle one or directly to the most expensive. Why?

Because in the vast array of options in e-commerce, price is a signal. And that signal communicates what no optimized description can convey: the product's level of effectiveness. For the buyer's brain, your self-perceived value is the best available evidence of your item's true quality. If you sell a "foolproof system" for the price of a coffee, the brain immediately assumes it's recycled information from the internet.

Signaling Theory on Digital Platforms

In saturated markets where the buyer cannot touch the physical product or verify the quality of the contents before paying for it, sellers use "costly signals" to demonstrate authority.

Charging a high price is a powerful signal and difficult to fake. Maintaining a premium price requires the product to work; otherwise, one-star reviews would wipe out the listing in days. The buyer's brain knows this.

The low price, on the other hand, can be set by anyone. And that's exactly what the buyer automatically concludes: "If this product promises such great results but costs so little, something must be wrong with it."

The Paradox of Mistrust in E-commerce

Here's the heart of this chapter: The low price, instead of lowering the barrier to purchase, raises it.

Consumer psychologists call it the mistrust paradox: the desperate attempt to make your product more accessible by lowering the price generates a suspicious response. It doesn't communicate accessibility; it communicates risk.

This is triggered like a nuclear alarm in these situations:

1. **Niche Products and Intangible Solutions:**If you sell a highly specialized work of nonfiction, software, or a design, the result isn't verified until after the product has been used. If price is your only visible differentiator, lowering it undermines your own authority.
2. **Below the algorithmic radar:**If the average price of premium products in your category in markets like Germany, France, or the United States is $20, and you enter the market charging $5, the buyer doesn't think they've found a bargain. They think your product is low-end.

The 3 toxic profiles attracted by the lowest price

Those who advocate the "cheapest" strategy ignore a documented pattern: charging low attracts the worst online shoppers, destroying your retention metrics and reviews.

- **The Hypercritical Bargain Hunter:**Precisely because they paid little, they assume the product has flaws and scrutinize it looking for the error. They're the kind of buyer who leaves scathing 1-star reviews for a simple formatting mistake that a premium buyer would ignore.
- **The Compulsive Returner:**They buy on impulse because "it's cheap," but at the first obstacle, they demand a refund, affecting your return rates and penalizing your account on the platform.

- **The Unfaithful:** They didn't choose your brand for the quality of your illustrations or your value proposition; they chose you for the price tag. The second a similar product appears with a 50-cent discount, they'll be gone without a second thought.

The Volume Trap (Mathematics to make your catalog profitable)

"What I lose in margin I make up for in volume." This phrase is the most dangerous myth of mass sales. It requires monumental traffic that is rarely free or sustainable.

Imagine the math behind your online catalog trying to generate $3,000 per month:

Variable	Scenario A (The Low Price Trap)	Scenario B (The Real Value Price)
Product Price / Net Royalty	$3.00	**$15.00**
Volume needed for the goal	1,000 sales per month	**200 sales per month**
Acquisition Cost (Advertising)	Extremely high. You need to get thousands of clicks.	**Controlled.** You can bid higher for quality conversions.
Management and Reviews	Manage complaints and queries from	**Monitor the satisfaction of a small, select group.**

Variable	Scenario A (The Low Price Trap)	Scenario B (The Real Value Price)
	1,000 different people.	

With one-fifth of the sales volume, you earn exactly the same amount of money. What do you do with the extra margins? You invest in robust advertising campaigns, pay for better keyword analysis tools, and improve the design of your future releases with advanced artificial intelligence tools.

The invisible cost of low margins

There's a tax that doesn't appear in any of your store's metrics, but that you pay every day: the cost of not being able to scale.

When your margins are minimal, your room for maneuver is nonexistent. You can't invest in pay-per-click marketing because the cost per acquisition eats up your small profit. You can't expand into international markets because you don't have the budget for professional translations. You're stuck relying on an unpredictable trickle of organic traffic.

Charging a fair price for the quality of your products is not greed; it is the mathematical requirement to be able to feed the advertising ecosystem that will grow your business sustainably.

Closing Exercise: Audit of your Catalog

Open your sales dashboard and check the numbers for your most popular products:

1. **Profitability audit:**Which product sells the most units and which one gives you the highest net margin? Often, they're not the same.
2. **The ideal scenario:**If you doubled the price of your "star" product, how many fewer sales could you afford to lose in order to still earn exactly the same amount of money at the end of the month?
3. **Review Analysis:**Check the reviews of your most affordable products versus your most expensive ones. Where are the complaints about minor details concentrated?

If the math confirms that massive volume at penny prices is drowning you in advertising costs without leaving any real profit, it's time to change your strategy.

Chapter 5: The Myth of the "Fair" Price

There is no target price. There is only the perceived price.

There's a phantom quest that consumes the time, energy, and profitability of thousands of product creators and e-commerce sellers every day: the search for the perfect price. That ideal price that no one questions in reviews and that the algorithm accepts without question. Here you'll discover why this quest is a deadly trap. The "perfect" price, as an objective concept in selling physical or digital products, simply doesn't exist. Understanding this will give you back absolute control over your profit margins.

The search that never ends

There's a limiting conversation that happens every time you're about to launch a new product or upload a new book to the platform.

It starts the moment you reach the "List Price" box. You research the market, look at what leading brands charge, analyze production or printing costs, and ask yourself the same old question:

How much should I really charge for this item?

You don't ask yourself, "How much do I want to earn per unit?" or "How much do I need to charge to invest in advertising and scale internationally?" You ask yourself, "How much should I charge?" As if there were a mathematically and morally correct answer waiting to be discovered. As if the market had the "true price" of your product on file and your only task was to guess it.

That question starts from a premise that seems obvious, but is completely false: the belief that there is a fair, objective price independent of who buys it.

The Illusion of Objectivity (The 100-Page Experiment)

The word "fair" implies a universal evaluation. Something is fair whether it benefits you or not. The problem is that the commercial value of a product doesn't work that way. Value is subjective. Always. Without exception.

What your product is worth to a buyer depends on their urgency, their context, and the severity of their problem. If value is subjective, then the "fair price" (which purports to reflect that value through costs) is a myth.

Let's illustrate this with something tangible. Imagine two physical books of exactly 100 pages each, printed on demand with the same paper quality, the same ink, and the same weight. Their manufacturing costs are identical to the penny.

- **Book A:** It is a collection of beautifully illustrated children's stories to read before bedtime.
- **Book B:** It is a technical and statistical manual with advanced systems for mastering the roulette and poker tables.

If production costs dictated the fair price, both should cost exactly the same. However, the reader of Book B is buying a strategy to multiply their money at a casino; a direct return on investment. The buyer of Book A is buying a moment of family connection. The perceived value and price elasticity of these two products are entirely different worlds.

The same applies to physical items. A fermented dough might be just $3 "fish food" to a weekend angler. But if that same formula is the secret to catching a heavy catfish in a competitive tournament, to a sport fisherman that dough is worth $30 without hesitation.

The value is not in the manufacturing materials; it is in the transformation of the one who consumes it.

The 4 Myths of Price Targets in Trading

The illusion of a "fair price" masquerades as financial logic. These are the four traps sellers fall into to justify cheap labels, and the psychological reality that debunks them:

The Myth of the Salesman	Apparent Logic	The Reality of the Consumer
1. Manufacturing Cost + Margin	*"I calculate my production/printing costs, add 30%, and that's my price."*	The buyer doesn't care about your logistics costs. They care about their own problem. If your product saves them hours of frustration, charging based on the ink or the plastic is just throwing money away.
2. The Price of the Algorithm	*"It's fair to charge the average price of the products that appear on the first page of search results."*	The "market" is not an objective judge. If you charge the average price, the algorithm classifies you as just another generic product. High-value products attract clicks because of their exclusivity, not their similarity.
3. As dictated by the Buyer	*"The fair price is the one the customer*	The anchor of "what's reasonable" comes from the customer's history of cheap purchases, not from the actual value of

The Myth of the Salesman	Apparent Logic	The Reality of the Consumer
	considers reasonable in their reviews."	your item. Never set prices to please the cheapest buyer.
4. Zero-Friction Pricing	*"There's a perfect price point where no one will leave a review complaining about the price."*	False. There will always be someone who returns a 50% off product because they consider it "expensive." Pursuing frictionless sales will lead you straight to bankruptcy.

If there's no target price, what is there?

There is perception. And perception in an online store or in a listing ecosystem has levers that you can systematically activate.

The difference between a product that always relies on discount coupons to sell and a premium item that sells at full price in international markets every day doesn't necessarily lie in the factory. It lies in a golden rule of commerce: Price isn't discovered. It's constructed.

The Perception Framework: 5 Elements to Build Your In-Store Price

If the price lives in the buyer's mind while they look at their screen, the strategy changes from "how much does it cost to manufacture this?" to "what does the customer need to see in this listing for the price to seem irrelevant?"

1. **The Transformational Narrative (Copywriting):**A descriptive bullet point is a cost. An SEO-optimized bullet point focused on the pain point is an investment.
   - *Evil:*"500-gram paste bait formula." (Read as an expense).
   - *Good:*"Hyper-fermented formula with olfactory attractants designed to ensure high-weight catches in murky waters." (Reads like the tournament win.)
2. **The Specific Social Proof:**Generic star ratings aren't enough. The brain needs to see real-world use cases. A listing that includes photos of users successfully using the product makes the price barrier disappear. Visual proof eliminates financial hesitation.
3. **Comparison Control (Keywords):**If you allow your product to rank for generic keywords, you'll be compared to dollar-dollar junk. Use data analytics tools to rank for "long-tail" keywords, where customers are looking for a premium, specialized solution.
4. **Total Congruence of the Packaging/Cover:**A price of $40 for a listing with a dark photo and no rich content (A+) is perceived as a rip-off. That same price with rendered images, usage diagrams, and a high-contrast cover is perceived as the industry standard.
5. **Zero Friction in the Shopping Experience:**Clarity of information. If the customer knows exactly what they will receive, how to use it, and what problems it will prevent, their "payment pain" threshold rises dramatically.

The liberation of letting go of "Justice"

Letting go of the myth of fair pricing is dizzying at first. It means you can no longer blame China's price war or platform saturation for your low margins. The responsibility for increasing perceived value is 100% yours.

But after the initial excitement comes freedom. You have real power over your margins. The metadata you configure, the cinematic quality of your covers, the optimization of your ad copy, and your brand authority are all assets you control.

One last truth: The Honest Price

There is no objectively fair price, but there is an honest price.

An honest price in e-commerce is one that genuinely reflects the quality and transformative value your product delivers. It's a price that allows your buyer to get great value, while providing you with the necessary margin to reinvest in advertising, improve your designs, and scale your catalog to multiple languages and borders.

The honest price isn't dictated by the competition on the front page. You dictate it. That price does exist. And that's the price you're going to start printing on your labels.

Chapter 6: Diagnosis: How Are You Setting the Prices of Your Products?

Self-assessment with included practical tool. The real starting point in digital commerce.

Neurological theory and cognitive biases are useless if you don't know exactly where your catalog's profitability is being bled away. In this chapter, we'll set neuroscience aside for a moment to audit your store or listing with the clinical precision of a surgeon. You'll discover which "Pricing Archetype" you currently belong to and apply the Profit Leakage Matrix to pinpoint where you're leaving margins on the table.

The end of algorithmic blindness

So far, we've deconstructed how your buyer's mind works when browsing the internet. You already know that price is a signal of quality, that the amygdala reacts to the design of your listing, and that selling cheaply often alienates the most committed buyers.

But knowing how the consumer's brain works is useless if you continue to operate your catalog on autopilot.

Most product creators, freelance authors, and e-commerce sellers suffer from strategic blindness. When an advertising campaign fails to convert, they blame the algorithm. When cost per acquisition (CPA) eats into profits, they blame market saturation. They almost never look at the true source of the problem: their own system for setting and maintaining the perceived value of their products.

To transform your pricing structure, you need a realistic starting point. And reality is measured by data and behavior, not intentions.

The 4 Pricing Archetypes in E-commerce (Which one describes you today?)

Before moving on to the numerical tool, identify your behavior pattern when launching a product. Read these four profiles with brutal honesty. Your goal isn't to feel good; it's to isolate the problem.

- **1. The Cost Calculator (Cost + Margin):**

  Add up the manufacturing or printing costs, the platform's logistics fees, and a 30% "ethical margin." The tragedy is that it completely ignores the value of transformation. If you've created a roulette system that can generate thousands of dollars in winnings for the reader, or an article that saves hours of work, you're still charging for it based solely on the cost of the paper or plastic.

- **2. The Algorithm Mirror (Direct Competition):**

  Their price is dictated by the first page of search results. They spend hours researching what other sellers charge and position their product exactly at the average. Their tragedy is that they become a commodity (a generic item). By not standing out in price or authority, they become invisible.

- **3. The Panic Offer (Self-Sabotage):**

  He launches a high-quality product and activates his ad campaigns (like Amazon Ads). If the product doesn't take off organically in the first three days, he panics. His first reaction is to cross out the original price and apply a permanent 50% discount. His tragedy is that he destroys his brand authority and trains the algorithm to send him only bargain-hunting buyers.

- **4. The Value Architect (The Objective):**

  It charges in direct proportion to the solution it delivers. It uses cinematic-lit homepages, structured metadata with long-tail keywords for international markets, and rich content (A+) to visually justify a premium price. It understands that a high price gives it the necessary margin to dominate advertising bids.

If you identified with the first three, you're not alone. It's the default behavior in mass commerce. But it's time to measure the real impact of that behavior.

The Practical Tool: Profit Leakage Matrix

Below, you will find a 10-question diagnostic test designed to identify the invisible cracks in your product catalog.

Instructions: Answer with a simple "YES" or "NO" based on your last six months of actual operation in listing, promoting, and selling your products.

No.	Operational and Sales Situation	Answer (YES / NO)
1	When an ad campaign doesn't convert immediately, is your first reaction to lower the product price instead of improving the copywriting and listing images?	
2	Are your current prices based primarily on calculating your production/printing costs plus a small fixed margin?	

No.	Operational and Sales Situation	Answer (YES / NO)
3	Did you set the price of your latest release simply by averaging what the first five competitors in the search results were charging?	
4	Have you ever felt frustrated seeing a highly specialized product you created competing for pennies against generic, low-quality copies?	
5	Do you rely heavily on free promotions, flash sales, or permanent discount coupons to maintain your positioning and sales volume?	
6	Do you have active listings without premium visuals (such as A+ content, 3D mockups, or cinematic-quality covers), and yet you wonder why they aren't selling for more?	
7	Are you terrified of raising your prices by 20% because you're convinced the algorithm will penalize you and your sales will plummet to zero?	
8	When a direct competitor in your niche lowers their price, do you feel an immediate urge to match their offer in order not to lose market share?	

No.	Operational and Sales Situation	Answer (YES / NO)
9	Do you spend more time worrying about your competitors' prices than researching the exact search intent of your buyers in different languages or markets?	
10	Do you think selling a massive volume of units with a minuscule profit margin is the only way to build a sustainable digital business?	

Brutal Results and Diagnosis

Add up the number of "YES" answers.

0 to 2 "YES" answers: Architect Level (Low Risk)

You have a firm grip on your positioning on the platform. You understand that price is a psychological anchor and you don't give in to pressure from cheap competitors. Your profit leakage is minimal. The following chapters will help you refine exclusivity and rarity tactics to maximize your profit margins.

3 to 5 "YES" answers: Intermediate Level (Stagnation Alert)

You're making money, but the cost of acquiring your ads is probably eating away at a large part of your profits. You have peaks of authority in your designs mixed with bouts of insecurity in your pricing strategy. You're leaving huge margins on the table for fear of testing the ceiling of your market.

6 to 8 "YES" answers: Critical Level (Structural Leak)

You're trapped in a war of attrition. You're actively attracting the fickle buyer who's only looking for the cheapest label. The problem isn't the quality of what you're selling (whether it's a wonderful children's series or a precise technical tool); the problem is that your digital presentation and metadata strategy are designed to compete in the low-end market.

9 or 10 "YES" answers: Emergency Level (Survival Mode)

Your amygdala is making all the decisions for your business. You're competing at rock bottom, and the profitability of your advertising campaigns is unsustainable. The good news is that, being at the lowest point of price leverage, simply optimizing the visuals of your listings and restructuring your narrative will boost your revenue almost overnight.

The insight you should take away from this diagnosis

Look at the questions you answered "YES" to. You'll notice an undeniable pattern: Almost all of them represent actions you take out of fear, not analytical strategy.

The fear of being hidden by the algorithm. The fear of not getting reviews. The fear of your product not being validated by the market.

The real diagnosis in this chapter isn't a number from 1 to 10. It's the absolute acceptance that the prices in your current listings are an exact reflection of your psychological limitations, not the limits of the international market. The market has money. The market pays premium prices every day for specialized solutions, simply because those who sell them present them with unwavering authority.

Chapter 7: The Anchor Effect (The First Number Always Wins)

How the brain uses the first visual digit as an absolute reference in e-commerce.

The human brain is incapable of evaluating a product's price in a vacuum. It always, without exception, needs a point of comparison to decide if something is expensive or cheap. This point of comparison is called an "anchor." The problem is that if you don't strategically place this anchor in your listing or online store before the user sees your price, they'll use the cheapest competitor's price. Here you'll learn to master the most powerful cognitive bias in pricing: whoever puts the first number on the screen controls the perception of the purchase.

The fear of the cognitive void on the internet

Imagine you're browsing an online store specializing in imported equipment and you see a carbon fiber fishing rod for $400.

Is it a bargain or are you being scammed?

Your brain panics for a split second. You have no way of knowing because there's a cognitive gap. You have no absolute point of reference. Your mind, desperate to make sense of the number, will search for any clue on the screen. If in the "Similar Products" section you see fishing rods for $1,200, suddenly $400 sounds like the best deal of your life. If the suggested products cost $50, you'll feel insulted.

The rod is the same. The number is the same. The only thing that changed was the number your brain processed for comparison.

This is the Anchoring Effect. It was documented by psychologists Amos Tversky and Daniel Kahneman (Nobel Prize in Economics), who discovered that when people try to estimate the value of something, they irrationally cling to the first piece of numerical information they receive, even if that information has no direct relation to the quality of the product.

The "Generic Search" Error

If you understand this bias, you'll realize that the way most sellers list their products on massive platforms (like Amazon KDP, Shopify, or MercadoLibre) leaves them at the mercy of the algorithm.

Imagine a buyer is looking for a technical book or a strategy manual. Your product costs $24.99. But the buyer arrived at your page after scrolling through five low-quality listings that cost $4.99.

What is the customer's mental anchor while reading your headline? $4.99.

When their eyes land on your price of $24.99, the gap between their (very low) anchor and your price is so large that their insula (the brain's pain center) lights up. Their automatic response will be: "Wow, that's really expensive."

It's not that your product isn't worth it; it's that you allowed the number to be evaluated against the wrong benchmark. You need to regain control of that number.

The 3 High-Conversion Anchoring Tactics for Products

For the Anchoring Effect to work for you, you need to strategically place high numbers in your customer's mind before or at the same time they see your actual price. Here are the three most effective tactical frameworks in digital commerce:

Tactic 1: Anchoring the Cost of the Problem (The Price of Failure)

The most powerful anchor you can use in your product page text isn't your price, but the money the customer is already losing. You need to force the customer to confront the financial "hemorrhage" they're experiencing by not having your product.

- **Practical Application:**Imagine you're selling an advanced manual on mathematical systems and probability for casino tables (roulette or poker). Before the customer can even decide if the $35 price tag is too much, you anchor your description with this key text: "Entering a poker table without understanding the math behind the game can easily cost you your $500 buy-in in a single 20-minute losing streak."
- **The Effect:**You've installed a $500 anchor. When your brain looks back at the book's price ($35), it no longer processes it as a printed piece of paper. It processes it as a low-cost protective shield against a $500 loss. The price is no longer high.

Tactic 2: List Price vs. Current Price (Visual Cross-Out)

It's the oldest tactic in e-commerce, but it still works because it exploits a direct flaw in the prefrontal cortex. It consists of displaying the suggested retail price (MSRP) crossed out, right next to the current selling price.

- **Practical Application:**In your store, you set the List Price to $59.99 (crossed out) and the Sale Price to $34.99.
- **The Effect:**The buyer isn't evaluating whether $34.99 is a fair price for the product. They're evaluating that they're making $25.00 on the transaction. The original anchor price ($59.99) makes the actual price feel like a personal win. (Note: Use ethically. The crossed-out price should represent the actual market value of similar products or the historical price of your item.)

Tactic 3: The "Top-Down" Model (The Catalog Ecosystem)

If you offer multiple versions of a product, multiple formats of a book (Kindle, Paperback, Hardcover) or bundles, the platform often allows you to display the options together.

The common mistake is highlighting the cheapest option to "attract" customers. You should do the exact opposite.

1. **First, present (or launch) your Premium Edition (The Anchor):**A $120 package that includes the physical product, extra accessories, or a deluxe format with color illustrations.
2. **Present your Standard Edition (Your real goal):**$29.99 dollars.

- **The Effect:**If the buyer first sees that the entire ecosystem costs $120, their brain adjusts to that price point. When they look at the standard $29.99 edition (the product you really wanted to sell in bulk), they no longer feel like they're paying too much; they feel like they're making a smart financial decision. If only the $29.99 version existed, it would have seemed expensive.

What to do about the "Similar Products" section

On massive platforms, you can't prevent the algorithm from showing your cheaper competitors right below your product. What's the neuro-strategic antidote? Visually anchoring your superior quality before users scroll.

Your main image and your metadata (title and subtitle) should establish an anchor of exclusivity.

- If you sell specialized fishing baits or attractants, your branding can't be just a plain white boat. It needs to be surrounded by trophies, high-performance seals, and a graphic label that says "Tournament Formula."
- If you're selling a children's book, the cover image should scream "high literature" through its typographic design and contrasts.

When a customer goes downstairs and sees the competition half-priced with generic packaging, their brain doesn't think, "I'm going to save money." It thinks, "This is just a cheap, low-quality version of what I just saw." You've just used your competition's mediocrity as an anchor to elevate your own value.

Tactical Execution Summary

Your task for this week is to audit your product listings and descriptions under the following three unbreakable rules of consumer neuromarketing:

1. **Rule 1:**Whoever calls out the first number controls the board. Build the numerical context (how much money or time is lost without the product) in the first lines of your description.
2. **Rule 2:**Leverage the visual anchoring power of multiple formats. If you have a product, create a premium version (a bundle, a hardcover edition) not just to sell it, but to serve as a protective anchor for the standard product.
3. **Rule 3:**If your customer doesn't feel the "cost of the problem," your product will always be an expense. Translate the buyer's frustration into a tangible number that justifies your price tag.

Chapter 8: Loss Aversion (Sell what the product prevents, not what it adds)

Losing $100 hurts more than gaining $100. Use this in your catalog descriptions.

The vast majority of product pages fail because they promise a bright and positive scenario, ignoring the fact that the human brain is biologically programmed to prioritize survival over ambition. Here you'll discover how to use the Loss Aversion bias to transform your items (even the most expensive ones) into an emergency rescue that the shopper feels compelled to add to their cart today.

The asymmetry of pain and pleasure in purchasing decisions

Imagine we flip a coin. If it lands on heads, I'll give you $100. If it lands on tails, you have to pay me $100 out of your own pocket. Do you accept the bet?

If your brain works like that of 90% of human beings, you will reject it immediately.

Mathematically, the bet is even (50/50). But neurologically, the scales are tipped. Psychologists have demonstrated with Prospect Theory that the pain of losing something is, on average, twice as intense as the pleasure of gaining the same amount. Losing $100 hurts far more than the joy of finding $100 on the street.

Our brains evolved in a hostile environment where losing the day's resources meant death, while finding extra resources only offered a small, temporary advantage. Survival always mattered more than thriving. And that same prehistoric brain is the one that today swipes its finger across an online store to decide whether to click the "Buy Now" button.

The mistake of selling the "bright future"

Knowing that the brain reacts with twice the intensity to a threat of loss, let's review how the copywriting of your current listings is written.

Your descriptive bullet points probably sound like this:

- *"With this product, you're going to improve your performance."*
- *"You'll achieve faster results."*
- *"You'll enjoy an incredible design."*

You're selling profits. You're selling a "bright future." And while that sounds very positive, it has a fatal flaw in e-commerce: the profit is optional. If your customer closes the tab and doesn't get that extra benefit, their life goes on exactly the same. It doesn't hurt. They're in their comfort zone, and comfort doesn't create a sense of urgency to buy.

But what if you shift the focus on your product page and show them what they're already missing out on by not having your item in their hands? Optionality disappears. Absolute urgency takes over.

The Hemorrhage Framework: How to Reframe Your Lists

To activate loss aversion, you must become a diagnostician. Your job is not to scare; it's to illuminate the money, time, energy, and frustrations the client is already experiencing.

Let's see how this neurological shift is applied in writing descriptions for different product niches:

The Product	Focus on Profit (Weak and Optional)	Focus on Loss (Urgent and Unforgettable)
Total Station / Surveying Equipment	"Perform highly accurate and fast land surveys for your infrastructure projects."	"Stop losing multi-million dollar bids due to millimeter errors. Avoid the catastrophic cost overruns caused by inaccurate leveling calculations during the foundation phase."
Premium Bait or Attractor for Sport Fishing	"Attract bigger fish with this highly effective fermentation formula."	"Don't go home empty-handed. Avoid wasting hundreds of dollars on fuel and specialized lake permits by using bait that large species ignore."
CAD Software / B2B Digital Tool	"Optimize your blueprint design and streamline your engineering team's workflow."	"You're wasting valuable team time by paying unnecessary overtime, simply because you're relying on slow software that's delaying the delivery of work sites."
Industrial Phone Case	"Protect your device with this modern design and ultra-resistant materials."	"A single slip on concrete will cost you $800 in screen repairs. Protect your work tool today."

The product you're sending is exactly the same in both columns. But in the right-hand column, the buyer feels like they have an open wound. And people don't argue about price tags when they're bleeding out.

The Cost of Inaction (COI) in E-Commerce

The secret weapon of loss aversion is a specific number: the Cost of Inaction (COI).

Before the customer judges whether the price of your product is high or low, you must force them to look squarely at how much it costs them to do nothing.

Imagine you're selling a $500 annual license for advanced construction supervision and monitoring software. The customer's prefrontal cortex will likely resist the initial expense. But if the description highlights that an error in asphalt or granular base control due to a lack of suitable software could result in a $15,000 penalty from the contractor, the scenario changes dramatically.

The mental narrative you construct in your product description is this:

- **Option A (Do not buy the product):**Extremely high risk of losing thousands of dollars in operating cost overruns or ruined materials.
- **Option B (Buy the product):**A one-time expense of $500 to stop that threat permanently.

Thanks to loss aversion, rejecting the product becomes neurologically unbearable. Your high price suddenly feels like very cheap insurance.

Risk Reversal: Calming the Amygdala Before the "Checkout"

There is one last critical detail in selling products: the buyer not only hates wasting time or money that he is already wasting in his daily life; he is also terrified of losing the money he is going to pay you if the item does not live up to its promises.

For this mental trigger to close high-value sales, you must visually absorb some of that fear on the page. This is called Risk Reversal.

If you sell at high prices, you can't force the customer to assume 100% of the risk. You must make guarantees the main focus of the area near the purchase button.

- *Guarantee of results/performance:*"Put this equipment to the test on your next project. If calibration doesn't reduce your data capture time by 30%, we'll give you your money back."
- *Physical quality guarantee:*"Immediate replacement, no questions asked, if the item suffers any structural damage during the first year of heavy use."

When you take the risk of making the wrong choice off the buyer's shoulders and put it on yours, their amygdala completely relaxes. Loss aversion is deactivated with respect to your price tag, and they focus solely on solving the problem that brought them to your page in the first place.

Tactical Execution Summary

1. **Audit your bullet points:**Review your current listings. Stop overselling the heavens. Growth and efficiency are nice concepts, but not urgent ones. Identify the exact pain point, financial risk, or technical frustration your buyer is experiencing today.
2. **Calculate the bleeding:**Translate that pain into tangible scenarios. How much money are you losing on the project? How many hours of fishing are you wasting? That's the Cost of Inaction (COI) that should headline your description.
3. **The perfect contrast:**Always present the benefits of your product as the antidote to IOC. Your product should feel like the ultimate tool that prevents the problem from getting worse.

4. **Highlights of the guarantee:**Eliminate the fear of online shopping by offering solid, visible, and clear guarantees right before the checkout cart. Those who charge more for a superior product must back it up with the strongest guarantees in the industry.

Chapter 9: The Decoy Effect (The Middle Package Always Sells)

The three-option trap and how to design it to your advantage in e-commerce.

Listing a product in your store with a single price tag is like playing Russian roulette with your conversions. It forces the shopper into a binary decision: "I buy it or I close the tab." Here, you'll learn how to hack that decision using the Decoy Effect, a pricing architecture tactic that eliminates the "don't buy" option and subtly guides the brain toward the most profitable bundle in your catalog, making them believe it was their own brilliant idea.

The single price listing error

Think about the last time you launched a physical or digital product. You uploaded the photos, wrote the description, and set a single price: $50.

What happens in the user's brain when they see that single number?

A binary and extremely dangerous question is triggered in trading: "Do I want to spend $50 on this item, YES or NO?"

In an online shopping environment filled with distractions and uncertainty, the human brain defaults to saying "NO" to protect its money (loss aversion). Furthermore, with only one price, the buyer has nothing to compare it to within your own store. To assess whether your $50 is fair, they'll be forced to search for similar products using the search bar or Google. You've just sent them straight into the clutches of your competition.

But what if, instead of a single price, you present three strategically structured options (such as bundles or variations)?

The brain's question changes drastically. It no longer asks, "Should I buy it or not?" Now it asks, "Which of these three should I get?"

You have just removed the "do not buy" option from the main focus of their attention.

The neuroscience of comparison (The Economist case)

The human brain is terrible at evaluating the absolute value of things in a vacuum, but it is a perfect machine at evaluating relative values (comparisons).

Researcher Dan Ariely demonstrated this with the famous experiment by The Economist magazine, which laid the foundation for pricing in modern commerce. The magazine offered three subscription options:

1. **Digital Subscription:$59**
2. **Print Subscription:$125**
3. **Digital + Print Subscription:$125**

Ariely tested this offer with her students. 84% chose option 3 (Digital + Print). 16% chose option 1 (Digital). Absolutely no one chose option 2 (Print only).

If no one chose option 2, Ariely decided to remove it to "simplify" the catalog. The options were as follows:

1. Digital Subscription: $59
2. Digital + Print Subscription: $125

What happened to sales? They were completely reversed. 68% chose the cheaper option ($59) and only 32% chose the more expensive one ($125). The company lost thousands of dollars in potential profit.

Why? Because the "Printed only for $125" option wasn't there to be purchased. It was there to be a visual lure.

The concept of Asymmetric Dominance in E-Commerce

The lure works thanks to a flaw in our mental software called asymmetric dominance bias.

When you present a buyer with two options (one cheap and basic, the other expensive and complete), the brain hesitates. It's a difficult decision because both have pros and cons. But when you introduce a third option (the decoy) that is blatantly inferior to the complete option but costs almost the same, the more expensive option instantly becomes an irresistible offer. The brain stops thinking about the expense and focuses on the "win" of having found a bargain in your own store.

How to Build Your Own Value Trap (3-Option Framework)

To apply this to selling your products (whether they're physical kits, book bundles, or software tools), you need to structure your listings into three strategic levels. Your goal is never to sell all three equally; your goal is to drive massive traffic to the most profitable option for you.

Let's do the exercise with a physical product, for example, a specialized kit (such as a surveying tool set or a complete sport fishing kit):

Supply Architecture	Option 1: The Basic (Low Anchor)	Option 2: The Lure (The Trap)	Option 3: The Premium (Your Goal)
The Hidden Purpose	Attract bargain hunters and establish the price floor.	**Make the Premium option seem like an absurd and**	**It's the product you really want to sell and where your net**

Supply Architecture	Option 1: The Basic (Low Anchor)	Option 2: The Lure (The Trap)	Option 3: The Premium (Your Goal)
		irresistible offer.	margin is perfect.
The Price	$45	$80	**$85**(Only $5 more than the Decoy)
Product Content	Main item only. No accessories, no case, standard version.	Main item + 1 minor accessory.	**Main item + Complete set of accessories + Premium hard case + Advanced guide.**
The Brain's Reaction	*"It's inexpensive, but it comes bare. I'll need to buy the accessories separately later."*	*"It comes with an accessory, but at $80 it doesn't seem like such a good deal in comparison."*	*"This is crazy! For only $5 more than the previous one, I get the complete luxury package. I'd be silly not to take advantage of it."*

Let's analyze the neurological trap:

- If you only showed the $85 Premium kit, the customer would compare it to $30 Chinese tools in other stores and think it was expensive.
- By offering the $80 lure (with a much lower value), the customer no longer compares your $85 with other stores. They compare it with your own $80.
- The customer doesn't choose the Premium package because it's cheap. They choose it because the mathematical framework you designed makes them feel like they're outsmarting the system and making the smartest decision possible.

The 3 fatal mistakes when designing your product lure

Many sellers try to implement the bundle strategy and fail because they make one of these three critical mistakes in their store architecture:

1. **Making the lure too attractive:**If the middle option conveniently solves the user's main problem, they'll buy it. The lure must be viable, but it must have a clear shortcoming (it's missing a key accessory, it doesn't have a case, it's a digital version instead of a physical one) that pushes the buyer toward the premium option.
2. **There is a significant price difference between the Lure and the Premium:**If the Basic costs $20, the Decoy $40, and the Premium $75, there's no decoy effect. The financial leap is too large. The price difference between the decoy and your ultimate goal should be small enough (just a few dollars) for the jump to seem obvious and justified ("For 10% more money, I get double the product").
3. **Add a fourth, fifth, or sixth variation:**The golden rule is number three. If you put six variations of color, size, and accessories on the same page, you trigger the Choice Paradox. Too many options overwhelm the prefrontal cortex. Faced with doubt and fatigue from evaluating so many

variables, the shopper will close the tab without adding anything to their cart.

Tactical Execution Summary

Your next product launch can't go to market with just one buy button. Starting today, you're going to design your pricing architecture using this mental model:

1. **Define your Margin Target:**Decide exactly which version of your product (the bundle or kit) you want to sell in bulk and set your ideal price (e.g., $65). This will be your Premium package.
2. **Create the Basic Anchor:**It offers a completely stripped-down version of the product at a price that will appeal to budget-conscious buyers (e.g., $35).
3. **Inject the Lure:**Design an intermediate package that lacks the most valuable accessories but price it uncomfortably close to your Premium (e.g., $59).
4. **Present and Be Silent:**Put all three options side by side on your product page and let the buyer's rational brain figure out for itself that the $65 Premium option is "the only logical and smart decision".

Chapter 10: The Rarity Bias (Rare Is Worth More)

Urgency, exclusivity, and limited availability ethically applied to the sale of products.

In the world of e-commerce and selling physical or digital products, having an "infinite inventory" doesn't communicate success; it communicates that your product is just another commodity. The human brain is biologically programmed to desire what is hard to obtain and undervalue what is abundant. Here you'll discover how to use Rarity Bias to transform your products into coveted items, increasing perceived value and accelerating cart sales without resorting to deceptive tactics.

The infinite inventory syndrome

Think about the last time you browsed an online store and found an interesting item. You looked at it, checked the price, liked it, but seeing that the store had unlimited availability, you thought, "I'll leave it in the cart and buy it next month."

That product has just become a victim of the infinite inventory.

In basic economics, this is known as the value paradox (diamonds versus water). Water is vital for survival, but it's cheap because it's abundant. Diamonds don't have a vital use, but they cost a fortune because they're scarce. In the market, you decide whether you're going to sell water or diamonds. And that decision is communicated through how you manage your inventory and your product launches.

The neuroscience of survival (FOMO in e-commerce)

The Rarity or Scarcity Bias is not a modern Shopify trick; it is an evolutionary survival mechanism.

In prehistoric times, if a resource was scarce (a food source), our brains released adrenaline and cortisol, compelling us to act immediately to secure it before someone else did. Today, our amygdala still reacts in the same way to a "Last Units" label.

When a buyer perceives that a product is running out, FOMO (Fear Of Missing Out) is activated. This trigger deactivates the logical procrastination of the prefrontal cortex ("let me think about it, I'll compare prices at another store") and activates the sense of emotional urgency ("I have to secure mine now or I'll lose it").

But this is where most online stores ruin the strategy: they confuse scarcity with lying.

The trap of false urgency (How to destroy your brand value)

The product market is infected with what analysts call Fake Scarcity.

- A generic countdown clock on the product page that magically resets when it reaches zero.
- A red text that says "Only 2 left in stock!" for a dropshipping product that comes from massive international factories.
- A constant pop-up that says "Someone in Madrid just bought this" generated by a bot.

Today's consumer is trained to spot these tactics immediately. When the customer's brain detects artificial scarcity, the insula registers outrage and a feeling of being deceived. Once you're perceived as a manipulative business, trust is broken and your brand value plummets.

Real product shortages must be logical, verifiable, and above all, ethical.

The 3 Pillars of Ethical Scarcity for Products (Application Framework)

To apply rarity to your catalog without losing elegance, you must structure your releases and availability around three verifiable axes.

Type of Shortage	How NOT to do it (Fake/Desperate)	How to do it (Ethically and with Authority)
1. Inventory Shortage (Lots/Drops)	Display a perpetual "Last 3 units" on a mass-produced product.	Create limited production batches. "Launch edition: Only 500 units of this series have been manufactured. Once sold out, the mold is retired."
2. Time Scarcity (Sales Windows)	A "Offer ends today" banner that remains active every day of the year.	Strategically withdraw the product from the market. "This special collection is only available during tournament season, from March 1st to 15th."
3. Scarcity of Access (Exclusivity)	Give an "exclusive" discount to everyone who visits the website.	Limit who can buy first. "48-hour early access exclusively for our VIP list subscribers, before opening the inventory to the general public."

Let's analyze the psychology behind correct axes with real-world scenarios:

- **Limit your inventory (The "Drop" model):**Imagine a store specializing in sport fishing equipment and supplies. If they sell a high-performance fermented bait formula and always have thousands in stock, the customer isn't in a hurry. But if they advertise a special batch of only 50 tubs prepared specifically for the peak tournament season, the inventory sells out in hours. The customer feels they're acquiring an exclusive competitive advantage.

- **Limiting time (The "Vault" model):**Disney dominated this for years by locking its films away and only releasing them for a few months at a time. If your product is only available for two weeks a year, consumers won't argue about the price.
- **Limiting access (The VIP model):**Imagine launching a new series of children's picture books. Instead of simply releasing the book on the platform with immediate worldwide availability, you offer a numbered, hardcover first edition only to readers who purchased the previous series. You reverse the sales dynamic: the customer feels privileged to have the right to buy.

How to inject weirdness into your product descriptions

The way you write your store copy is vital. Never use excessive capitalization or unnecessary exclamation marks.

Example for a premium product sheet:

"This item has been designed with rigorous technical specifications and high-density materials. Due to our thorough quality control, our production capacity is limited to batches of 200 units per quarter."

We are currently shipping Batch #04. If the purchase button is active, it means there are still units available for immediate shipment. If it appears grayed out, we invite you to join the waiting list for Batch #05 next quarter.

Look at what you just did:

1. You logically justified why there are few (quality control, meticulous process).
2. You gave the product a collector's status (Lot #04).
3. You demonstrated complete detachment by calmly informing him that, if it runs out, he will simply have to wait three months.

The fast-acting physical bond

If you have a large volume of inventory that you need to move quickly without lowering the base price of the product, the best way to apply ethical scarcity is to limit additional bonuses, not the core product.

- *"The main item will always be part of our permanent catalog. However, the first 100 orders this month will include a free hard-shell travel case and a printed advanced optimization manual. After the 100th order, the case will be sold separately at its regular price."*

The urgency to check out is real, the numerical limit is verifiable, and the customer feels an immediate impulse to act in order to get the maximum possible value.

Tactical Execution Summary

Before your next launch or redesign of your online store, apply these three iron rules:

1. **Kill the flat inventory:**Avoid making your best products seem endless. Create variations, seasonal editions, or limited-edition special packaging to inject collectability and a real sense of urgency.
2. **Reward loyalty with exclusivity:**Never release your best titles to the general public from day one. Create "waiting lists" or "VIP clubs" where the only way to get early access is with an email address.
3. **Justify the scarcity:**The brain needs a logical reason to believe that only a few units remain. If there are only a few left, explain why (hard-to-obtain materials, artisanal manufacturing, seasonal demand spikes). The reason validates the urgency.

Chapter 11: The Odd Price and the Magic of 9

$997 vs $1,000. When it works and when it destroys your positioning.

You've spent your whole life seeing prices ending in 9. They've been taught to you as the ultimate marketing trick. However, in the ecosystem of high-value services and premium digital businesses, blindly applying the "rule of 9" can be the most serious communication mistake you can make. Here, you'll learn exactly how your customer processes odd numbers, and when using $997 is a masterstroke or brand suicide compared to a resounding $1,000.

The oldest (and most misunderstood) trick in the market

Open any online store, look at a mall window display, or check the ads on your social media. The numerical landscape is monotonous: $9.99, $49, $199, $997.

This practice, known as charm pricing, is so ingrained in global commerce that many entrepreneurs, agency owners, and consultants apply it automatically. They finish their service proposal, calculate the value at three thousand dollars, and immediately change it to $2,997, thinking, "That makes it look cheaper, and I'll get more sales."

It's a conditioned reflex. And like any reflex applied without strategy, sometimes it works, but many other times it backfires on the user.

To master pricing architecture, you must stop copying what the supermarket does and understand what really happens in your customer's neurons when faced with a number ending in 9 versus a round number.

The neuroscience of the "Left Digit Effect"

The human brain reads and processes numbers from left to right. But it doesn't process them like a computer; it processes them with urgency and cognitive laziness.

When your customer sees a price of $997, their brain doesn't wait to read the last two digits to form an opinion. It immediately focuses on the leftmost digit: the 9. Even though the difference from $1,000 is a negligible three dollars, the brain emotionally categorizes $997 as "nine hundred" rather than "one thousand."

This phenomenon is called the Left Digit Effect. It drastically reduces the perception of "payment pain" because the psychological jump from 3 to 4 figures (from hundreds to thousands) feels massive.

If science says that $997 is perceived as significantly cheaper than $1,000, logic would dictate that you should always use the 9. But this is where high-level sales psychology takes an unexpected turn.

You don't always want your service to look cheap.

The dichotomy: Logical Purchases vs. Emotional Purchases

Researchers Monica Wadhwa and Kuangjie Zhang discovered a fascinating pattern in consumer behavior: round numbers and precise/odd numbers activate completely different brain circuits.

1. **The Rational Circuit (Odd Prices):**Prices like $97, $499, or $997 force the brain to perform a micro-calculation. Because they aren't "clean" numbers, they activate the prefrontal cortex (logic). The brain assumes that this number is the result of a highly refined calculation. It communicates: "This is a bargain," "This is a discount," "This is the best possible financial deal."
2. **The Emotional Circuit (Round Prices):**Clean prices like $1,000, $5,000, or $10,000 are processed with complete ease. They require no cognitive effort. They feel "complete" and

are processed in the limbic system (emotions). A round number communicates: "This is absolute quality," "This is premium status," "This is safe."

When the number "9" destroys your ranking

Imagine you are the director of a company about to hire an external consultant to solve a structural crisis that is costing you half a million dollars a year.

The consultant presents a flawless proposal. He projects authority, methodology, and results. When we get to the final slide about the investment, the number reads: $9,997.

In a split second, the carefully constructed authority falters. The director's brain detects an inconsistency. If this consultant is a business surgeon, why is he using late-night infomercial tricks to scrape together a sale? Why does he need to give me back $3 in change on a $10,000 transaction?

In B2B services, high-level consulting, or agencies that sell deep transformation, the number 9 conveys need. It screams "discount." And nobody wants to buy a discounted parachute.

When you sell at premium prices, your client isn't looking for the cheapest option; they're looking for the safest and most prestigious one. A price of $10,000 conveys unwavering confidence. It silently says, "My service is worth exactly this much. I don't need to manipulate your perception with pennies."

When the "9" or the "7" is your best weapon

Dismissing charm pricing would be a huge mistake. It's devastatingly effective, but only in the right environments.

Odd pricing works like magic when sales volume, purchase friction, or product format demand it:

- **Information Products and Digital Courses:**A video-recorded program priced at $997 sells exponentially better than one priced at $1,000. Why? Because in mass-market digital education, users are looking for the feeling of having taken advantage of a deal, and the three-figure barrier ($997 instead of $1,000) keeps the product within the realm of "justifiable impulse purchases."
- **Subscriptions and Software (SaaS):**Paying $49 a month has a much higher conversion rate than $50. With recurring expenses, the brain accumulates the pain month after month. The Left Digit Effect here is a necessary anesthetic.
- **Scalable B2B Services or Entry Audits:**If you sell a standardized "product" service (e.g., an initial technical audit), using a price like $497 reduces friction for a cold customer to open their wallet for the first time.

The Decision Framework: Round vs. Precise

From today onwards, your pricing will no longer be based on a mathematical hunch. You'll apply this decision matrix to determine exactly which numerical format to use in your proposals:

Price Type	Numeric Format	When to Use It	What the Customer Perceives
The Price of Charm	$97 / $497 / $997	Information products, subscriptions, low and medium ticket prices, mass e-commerce.	*"It's a good deal. It's a bargain calculated to my advantage."*
The Surgical Price	$4,235 / $12,860	Highly customized B2B projects (custom web development, long	*"The supplier analyzed every variable of my project. It's an exact calculation of*

Price Type	Numeric Format	When to Use It	What the Customer Perceives
		technical implementations).	*hours and resources."*
The Prestige Price	$1,000 / $5,000 / $25,000	Elite consulting, premium agency retainers, status services and high-value transformation.	*"It's a mark of authority. They know their worth and they don't apologize for it."*

(Technical note: In surgical pricing, using non-rounded and seemingly random numbers—such as $4,235 instead of $4,200—disarms price objections in customized corporate proposals. The client feels it is impossible to bargain with a number that was calculated so meticulously.)

Tactical Execution Summary

1. **Audit your current catalog:** If you're selling an agency service, direct coaching, or deep transformation consulting that costs over $1,000, remove the 9s and 7s from your final proposal. Switch to round numbers today. You'll gain instant authority.
2. **Align friction with emotion:** If the goal is for the customer to buy quickly, with a single click and without speaking to you (digital products), use $997. If the goal is for the customer to trust your method after a one-on-one meeting, use $1,000.
3. **Do not mix numeric languages:** If your initial offer includes a very high anchor price (e.g., $10,000) and you then offer a more affordable package, don't break the consistency by

lowering it to $2,997. Maintain the prestige format and set it at $3,000. The aesthetic consistency of the number reinforces your brand positioning.

Chapter 12: The Halo Effect (Your Image Sets Your Price)

The visual perception of your brand determines how much you can be paid.

There's a mental shortcut in the human brain that automatically links outward beauty with inner quality. It's called the Halo Effect. In product marketing, this cognitive bias dictates that impeccable packaging, cinematic-quality photography, or superior listing design mathematically justify a higher price. Here, you'll learn why design isn't just decoration, but your most profitable selling point.

The millisecond trial

Imagine you're browsing the internet looking for wireless headphones. You find two options that have exactly the same audio specifications, the same battery life, and the same internal chip.

- **Product A ($25 dollars):**The main photo is slightly pixelated, the background isn't completely white, the logo looks like it was made in five minutes, and the description has a minor spelling mistake.
- **Product B ($120 dollars):**The main image is a hyper-realistic 3D render with perfect lighting. The logo conveys minimalism, the typography on the box is elegant, and the website loads instantly with smooth animations.

On a rational level, Product B does exactly the same thing as Product A. However, the consumer's brain doesn't operate rationally. Upon seeing Product B, the buyer immediately assumes that the sound will be superior, the materials more durable, and the warranty more reliable.

They pay almost five times more for the same specifications. Why? Because the external image positively influenced their judgment of the internal quality.

The neuroscience of beauty: The Halo Effect

In 1920, psychologist Edward Thorndike discovered a fascinating flaw in the way humans evaluate others. He noticed that if a person possessed a highly prominent positive trait (such as being physically attractive), evaluators automatically assumed that they were also intelligent, kind, and honest, without any evidence to support this.

This cognitive bias is known as the Halo Effect ("beautiful is good"). The brain is lazy; instead of analyzing all variables independently, it takes the strongest impression (the visual one) and extends it to the rest of the set.

In the retail of physical and digital products, the Halo Effect is precisely why brands like Apple can charge obscene profit margins on hardware that, piece by piece, costs a fraction of its retail price. The weight of the box, the texture of the cardboard, the millimeter-perfect slide when opening the packaging... the entire visual ecosystem screams "perfection." And if the box is perfect, the brain assumes the motherboard is too.

The Horns Effect: How carelessness destroys your profit margin

Unfortunately, the Halo Effect also works in reverse. It's known as the Horns Effect. If a single visual detail of your product or listing conveys mediocrity, the buyer's brain will extend that mediocrity to the entire item.

- You're selling a digital course with revolutionary content, but the video was recorded with a laptop microphone and there's an echo in the room. The buyer assumes the information is worthless and demands a refund.
- You sell a highly effective sport fishing bait, but you ship it in a generic plastic bag sealed with a staple. The customer assumes it's an amateur product and won't pay a premium price for it.
- You're selling a book with an advanced mathematical system, but the cover typography is stretched and the margins are

misaligned. The reader assumes the method inside is just as messy.

Online, your customer can't touch, smell, or taste your product before swiping their card. The image isn't the packaging of your product; at the point of sale, the image IS your product.

The Halo Framework: 3 Pillars to Increase Your Perceived Price

For this cognitive bias to work in your favor and justify high price tags in your catalog, you must secure three levels of your visual presentation:

Level of Impact	The Common Mistake (Kills the Margin)	The Halo Execution (Price Increase)
1. Photography and Renders	Photos taken with a phone, with poor lighting, noisy backgrounds, or harsh shadows.	Images with studio lighting, hyper-realistic mockups, and 3D renderings that show microscopic textures and details.
2. Typographic Identity and Copy	Use of multiple free fonts, piled-up text, and boring descriptive language.	Clear visual hierarchy. Typefaces selected to convey luxury or technology. Texts formatted with clean bullet points and strategic bolding.
3. The Unboxing Experience	The product arrives in a generic recycled cardboard box, with	The digital product is delivered through a private and intuitive dashboard. The physical product arrives in custom packaging, with a

Level of Impact	The Common Mistake (Kills the Margin)	The Halo Execution (Price Increase)
	no notes or clear instructions.	thank-you note on high-quality textured paper.

The illusion of "intrinsic quality"

Many creators and sellers get frustrated because they know their product is superior to the competition's, but they see the competitor selling ten times more while charging twice as much.

They tell themselves: "My formula is better," "My code is cleaner," "My material is more resistant."

The harsh reality of the market is that a product's intrinsic quality doesn't exist until the customer uses it. During the buying process, the only quality that matters is "perceived quality." And perceived quality depends entirely on the aesthetics of your listing, the strength of your brand, and the friction of your purchase process.

If your product is a 10/10 but your packaging and website are a 4/10, in the eyes of the market your product is a 4/10. Your price tag will be tied to that number.

Your brand is a cognitive shortcut

When you build a consistent Halo Effect around all the items in your store, something magical happens: your own brand becomes the anchor.

You no longer need to convince customers of the value of your next launch. When you release a new product, buyers will automatically assume it's extraordinary simply because it bears your logo. The Halo Effect transfers the authority built in the past to your new item.

Trust becomes your most valuable asset. And in digital commerce, trust is built from the ground up.

Tactical Execution Summary

1. **Audit your shop window:**Open your store's homepage or product listing as if you were a complete stranger. Identify the weakest visual element (a pixelated thumbnail? an outdated banner?). That element is lowering the price ceiling for your entire catalog. Remove it or improve it today.
2. **Invest in the packaging:**Whether physical or digital, the packaging justifies the profit margin. Hire a professional to create 3D renderings of your products, design cinematic covers, and ensure that the customer's first visual impression screams "premium."
3. **Maintain consistency:**The Halo Effect requires total consistency. If your cover is elegant, your description should have an elegant tone, and your purchase confirmation email should be elegantly formatted. A single visual flaw breaks the spell.

Chapter 13: The Buyer's Confirmation Bias

Your customer already made a decision before clicking. How to nurture that decision.

We believe consumers evaluate products objectively, weighing the pros and cons before reaching for their credit card. Neuroscience shows this is a fantasy. In the vast majority of online purchases (especially high-value or niche ones), the shopper has already made an instinctive, emotional decision before even reading your listing. Here, you'll discover how to use Confirmation Bias to deliver precisely the "logical ammunition" their brain needs to justify the purchase they already want to make.

The illusion of rational buying

Imagine a sport fishing enthusiast scrolling through their phone. They've had a rough time in their recent tournaments and are desperate for a change. Suddenly, they see your product thumbnail: a hyper-fermented bait formula with a premium price tag and dark, almost tactical packaging.

The image, the high price, and the exclusive design activate his limbic system. In a millisecond, his emotional brain says, "This is exactly what I need to win the trophy this weekend."

The purchase decision has just been made.

But he still hasn't clicked the "Add to Cart" button. Instead, he goes to the product page and starts scrolling, obsessively reading the technical description, the ingredients, and the reviews.

What is he really doing? He's not looking for "the truth." He's not evaluating options neutrally. He's looking for evidence that confirms the emotional decision he's already made, and he's actively ignoring any information that tells him otherwise.

This flaw in human software is called Confirmation Bias.

The brain as defense attorney

Psychologist Jonathan Haidt uses a brilliant analogy to explain how we process information: the emotional brain is a huge elephant, and the rational brain (the prefrontal cortex) is the small rider riding on it.

We think the rider is in control, but when the elephant decides to go to one side (whether out of desire, fear, or instinct), the rider doesn't have the strength to stop it. So what does the rider do? He starts inventing brilliant excuses to explain to others why going in that direction was an excellent idea from the start.

In e-commerce, your buyer acts like a defense attorney. Once their "elephant" falls in love with your product (due to the Halo Effect, scarcity, or visual price anchoring), their "rider" gets to work. They'll search for any fact, vignette, or review on your site to build a legal case justifying the purchase.

Your job in the product listing isn't to convince the elephant (the first impression already did that). Your job is to give the rider legal arguments.

How to feed the Confirmation Bias in your catalog

If you know that your buyer comes to your page desperately looking for reasons to say "yes," your sales copywriting should be structured to deliver that ammunition on a silver platter.

Here are the three categories of "ammunition" that the rational brain needs to justify an impulsive or high-value purchase:

1. Justification of Return on Investment (The Financial Argument)

Nobody wants to feel like a spendthrift or a compulsive shopper. The user needs to be able to tell themselves (or their spouse) that this purchase is, in fact, a smart save.

- **If you sell an advanced manual of systems for roulette or poker:**The buyer has already emotionally visualized themselves winning at the casino. Confirmation bias needs mathematical logic. The answer: "This system costs the equivalent of two lost hands at the low blinds table. By applying the probability matrix in your first session, the book pays for itself before the night is over."
- **The Effect:**The rational brain breathes a sigh of relief. The "expensive" purchase has just been reclassified as an "immediate return investment."

2. The Justification of Durability and Quality (The technical argument)

When a product costs more than the store average, the buyer needs technical details, however tedious they may seem, to justify the extra expense. They won't read them thoroughly, but they need to know they're there.

- *Ammunition:*Include cross-sectional diagrams, high-density bills of materials (e.g., "aerospace-grade aluminum"), or explain the rigorous 5-step quality control process for your product.
- **The Effect:**The buyer isn't a materials engineer, but upon seeing the dense technical specifications, his confirmation bias validates his instinct: "It makes sense that it costs $150. Look at all the technology inside."

3. The Justification of Identity (The Status Argument)

Humans buy physical and digital products to confirm the identity they wish to project to the world. The buyer chooses your premium item because they want to feel like a professional, not a novice.

- *Ammunition:* Write the text assuming the client belongs to an elite group. For example, "Designed exclusively for high-performance competitors who don't leave their results to chance" or "For parents who demand a higher standard in their children's cognitive development."
- **The Effect:** The buyer reads this and their brain confirms: "I am a serious competitor (or a great dad), therefore, this product is exactly what I should buy."

The danger of "cognitive dissonance" (How to lose a closed sale)

There's a lethal way to ruin confirmation bias, and many product creators unwittingly fall into this trap when setting up their stores. It's called cognitive dissonance, and it happens when you present the buyer with information that violently contradicts a decision they've already made.

Imagine a buyer enters your listing ready to purchase your flagship $100 product because the cover image and visuals project massive authority. They're looking for the "logical ammunition" in your description. But then, on the same page, you offer a flashing red banner with a 60% discount and text that reads "Total Clearance due to lack of stock!"

Neurological short circuit.

The elephant wanted status. The rider was looking for technical justifications. And you just shouted that your product is stagnant clearance merchandise. Confirmation bias breaks down, trust plummets, and the buyer abandons their cart because what they read doesn't match their initial feelings.

Your message, your price, your images, and your guarantees should always point in a single direction so that the brain flows smoothly towards the cash register.

Chapter 14: Pricing Based on Value, Not Cost

The formula to calculate what your service or product is really worth.

The moment you open a spreadsheet to add up your working hours, your operating costs, and then add a 30% "ethical markup" is the moment you've decided to limit your growth forever. Here you'll discover why charging for what it costs you to produce is detrimental to your own efficiency, and you'll learn the exact equation for setting prices based on the only number that matters to your customer's brain: their return on investment.

The spreadsheet error (Cost-Plus Pricing)

Imagine you are an elite cardiovascular surgeon. A patient arrives with a life-threatening blocked artery. It takes you exactly 45 minutes to perform the procedure to save him, because you have spent 20 years perfecting your technique.

If you applied the Cost-Plus Pricing model, your invoice would look like this:

- 45 minutes of your time at an hourly rate.
- Cost of surgical materials (scalpel, gauze, anesthesia).
- A 20% profit margin.

The patient would end up paying a pittance to save their own life. Even worse: if you were a novice, clumsy surgeon who takes six hours to perform the same operation and makes mistakes requiring more gauze and anesthesia, you'd charge much more!

Charging by cost or by the hour is a model that penalizes mastery.

In the world of B2B services, agencies, and consulting, it works exactly the same way. If you've created a lead generation system, a technical audit, or a sales funnel that you can implement in two days because you're an expert, charging for the hours it took you to create it is financial suicide.

Your client doesn't care about your sweat. They don't care how much you pay in office rent or how many hours you spend in front of the monitor. They care about only one thing: where they were before hiring you and where they'll be afterward.

The Real Value Equation

To move from cost-based pricing to value-based pricing, we need to stop guessing and start calculating. Consumer neuroscience and behavioral economics tell us that buyers always make an internal (unconscious) calculation before accepting a price.

We can structure that brain calculation into a tangible mathematical equation:

$$V = \frac{I_f + I_e}{R_p + E}$$

Where:

- V **(Perceived Value):** What the customer feels they are buying.
- I_f **(Tangible Financial Impact):** How much extra money will you earn or how much money/time will you save?
- I_e **(Intangible Emotional Impact):** Status, tranquility, elimination of stress or frustration.
- R_p **(Perceived Risk):** The fear that your solution won't work and they'll lose their money.
- E **(Effort and Friction):** How much work does the client have to do on their own to see results?

To charge premium rates, your goal is not to artificially increase your price, but to maximize the numerator (Impact) and reduce the denominator (Risk and Effort) to almost zero.

Step 1: Quantify the Financial Impact (I_f)

Never present a price without first doing the math with your client.

Let's say you have an agency and your service is to optimize the conversion rate (CRO) of an e-commerce business.

1. **The Diagnosis:** You discover that your prospect's store bills $50,000 per month, but its cart abandonment rate is 70% due to poor design.
2. **The Projection:** Your work can reduce that abandonment rate by 50%. That means recovering an extra $10,000 per month in sales that are currently being lost.
3. **The Financial Impact:** Your service will generate an extra $120,000 for him in the next year.

That's your I_f. The value of your service isn't the 40 hours you'll spend programming. The value of your service is $120,000 annually.

Step 2: The 10x Rule (Setting the Price)

Once you have quantified the financial impact you will generate or the money you will save your client, setting the price becomes an exercise in pure business logic.

This is where the 10x Rule comes in: For your customer's brain (their prefrontal cortex) to justify the purchase without hesitation, the perceived Return on Investment (ROI) should ideally be 10 times greater than your price.

- If you're going to generate $120,000 in value for it in one year...
- Your fair and ethical price is $12,000.

When you present a client with a $12,000 proposal and mathematically demonstrate that this investment will yield a $120,000 return, your service has essentially become free in their mind. You're asking them to give you a $10 bill in order to give them back a $100 bill.

If you charge only $1,000 out of fear, you're giving away your potential profit. If you charge $50,000, the equation breaks down, and the perceived risk stops the sale. A 10:1 ratio (or at least 5:1 in lower-margin industries) is the neurological sweet spot where the sale closes itself.

Step 3: Decrease the Denominator (Risk and Effort)

You can promise a financial impact of one million dollars, but if your client feels there is a 90% chance that you will fail them (High Risk), or that they will have to work 20 hours a week to implement your system (High Effort), the Perceived Value (V) plummets and they will ask for a discount.

How do you reduce the denominator to defend your premium rate?

Denominator Variable	How you ruin it	How to reduce it to zero (Armor)
Perceived Risk (R_p)	*"We will do our best to increase your sales."*	**Conditional Guarantees:**"If we don't increase your revenue by 15% in the first 90 days, we'll work month 4 for free until we achieve it." (Risk reversal).
Effort (E)	*"I will give you an 80-page PDF with the audit for your team to implement."*	**"Done-For-You" model:**"My team integrates with your platform, writes the texts, changes the code, and delivers

Denominator Variable	How you ruin it	How to reduce it to zero (Armor)
		the turnkey system to you. You just approve it."

Premium clients don't pay you more for more tasks. They pay you more for their time. The less effort your solution requires from the client, the more you can (and should) charge.

How to apply this if you sell intangibles (Consulting, Coaching, Design)

It's easy to calculate the return on investment (ROI) when you sell marketing or sales. But what if you sell brand design, corporate leadership consulting, or a service where the return isn't immediately monetary?

This is where Intangible Emotional Impact (I_e) comes in. You have to monetize the pain.

Ask your prospect:

- *"How much is the high staff turnover costing them because the leaders don't know how to communicate?"*(Recruitment costs, lost training time).
- *"How many corporate clients haven't called you back because when they visit your website, the design makes them feel like you're a novice company?"*

Force your client to put a number on the intangible problem. Once they verbalize that their poor brand design is costing them premium clients, you have the number against which to anchor your price.

Chapter 15: How to Design Irresistible Packages

Three-level structure with psychological logic in each layer.

Giving your buyer complete control by presenting them with dozens of à la carte options is the fastest way to lose a sale due to analytical paralysis. On the other hand, offering only one option triggers the instinct to reject. The answer lies in bundling architecture. Here you'll learn to design a three-tiered ladder where each option serves a specific neurological purpose, invisibly guiding your customer toward the package you always wanted to sell them.

The danger of the open menu and decision fatigue

Imagine walking into a fancy restaurant and the waiter hands you a 40-page menu with hundreds of ingredients, asking you to create your own dish from scratch. Instead of feeling empowered, you'd feel overwhelmed. Your brain would burn so much glucose trying to calculate the perfect combination that you'd end up ordering the safest, cheapest option, or worse, leaving the restaurant altogether.

In the sale of digital products, books, or physical goods, the same thing happens. When you force the buyer to build their own cart by choosing each item individually, you trigger Decision Fatigue. The prefrontal cortex becomes overwhelmed trying to assess the risk of making a mistake.

Today's buyers don't want more choices; they want clarity and direction. They want an expert to have done the heavy lifting and come up with packaged solutions. And the magic number for the human mind to process options without becoming overwhelmed is three.

The Anatomy of the Three Levels

Designing bundles isn't simply about randomly combining three products and adding up their prices. It's an exercise in psychological architecture. Each level in your offering (Basic, Premium, Elite) has a specific function to fulfill. You don't expect to sell all three equally; in fact, two of those levels are simply contrasting tools to make the third shine.

Let's look at the underlying logic behind each layer:

Packaging Level	The Psychological Role	The Price	What's Included (The Value)
Level 1: The Basics(The Filter)	Attract the impulsive, low-budget buyer and anchor the transaction floor.	Profitable, but with little margin.	It partially solves the problem or requires a lot of effort and time from the customer.
Level 2: The Premium(Your Goal)	Be the "obvious" choice. It's the **package you design to sell in massive volumes.**	Slightly superior to the Basic one, but with a massive jump in value.	**The complete solution. Fast, frictionless, and with the best elements from your catalog.**
Level 3: The Elite(The Anchor)	Make the Premium package look cheap by contrast. Appeal to the 5% of buyers who	Asymmetrically high (3 to 5 times more than the Premium).	All of the above plus total exclusivity (e.g., limited editions, direct access, premium

Packaging Level	The Psychological Role	The Price	What's Included (The Value)
	demand absolute luxury.		physical format).

Practical Application: From Theory to the Showcase

To understand how these packages are built regardless of your niche, let's see how this architecture is applied in different high-profitability product lines.

Example 1: Technical and Strategic Niche

Let's say you publish high-end instructional content and manuals. You sell a complete probability and mathematics system for casino games.

- **Basic Level (The Filter - $29):**The main manual is in digital format (Mastering Roulette). The client has the information, but must create their own spreadsheets to play and study independently.
- **Premium Level (The Target - $59):**The complete series includes roulette strategy and poker volumes, plus ready-to-use automated calculation templates. The price increase is small, but the value gain is enormous. The customer doesn't hesitate.
- **Elite Level (The Anchor - $299):**The entire hardcover library, delivered to your home, plus access to a private community of advanced players and an extensive technical glossary.

Upon seeing the $299 package, the buyer's brain rationalizes that getting all the digital knowledge for $59 is the steal of the century.

Example 2: Children's Niche and Entertainment

Imagine you manage a series of illustrated children's books, such as Magical Tales to Dream About. The goal is to increase the average order value (AOV) for each parent who visits your store.

- **Basic Level ($15):**A single book in the series, available in paperback.
- **Premium Level ($45):**The complete five-volume collection in a gift box. The father feels he has his sleep routines sorted for the coming months.
- **Elite Level ($120):**The collection of hardcover books, plus audiobooks narrated with immersive artificial intelligence voices and sound effects for listening in the car.

The Elite Tier establishes your brand's status. The parent who was only going to spend $15 feels foolish for not getting the entire collection for $45. The Premium Tier wins again.

The 3 Irresistibility Triggers

For your Premium (Level 2) package to achieve massive conversions, it must contain three psychological elements that deactivate any objections in the buyer's mind:

1. **The Promise of Speed:**The package must explicitly promise that the customer will reach their goal faster than if they bought the items separately. The brain always pays more for time shortcuts.
2. **The "Missing Piece" Effect:**When putting together your package, don't just offer "more of the same." Group complementary products together. If you're selling a tool, package it with an advanced user manual. The customer will feel that buying the tool alone would leave the job incomplete.
3. **Package Name:**Never call them "Package 1, 2, and 3." The names should dictate the identity the buyer wants to assume.

Use titles like The Starter Kit, The Professional's Arsenal, or The Ultimate Collection.

The antidote to the paralyzed buyer

When you offer these three levels clearly, you eliminate the biggest friction in online commerce: forcing the customer to think.

Instead of making the buyer figure out which products go well together, you're telling them: "I've analyzed this problem thousands of times. This is the cheapest way to solve it halfway, this is the most exclusive way to solve it with luxury, and this is the smartest, fastest, and most efficient way to achieve exactly what you want."

The human brain, biologically designed to conserve energy and avoid danger, will take the middle path almost every time.

Tactical Execution Summary

Before publishing your next offer or redesigning your catalog, apply this pricing architecture filter:

1. **Identify your "Hero":** Select the product or bundle that gives you the highest profit margin and delivers the best results for your customers. Place it in Level 2 (Premium).
2. **Build the roof:** Create an outrageously complete and exclusive version of that same product. Price it so high it makes even you nervous. This will be your Level 3 (Elite). Its sole purpose is to make Level 2 seem accessible.
3. **Unveil the product:** Strip your flagship product of all accessories, bonuses, and perks. Leave it in its rawest, most economical form. This is your Level 1 (Basic).
4. **Visual alignment:** In your store, visually highlight the Premium Tier. Label it "Most Popular" or "Best Value" and make the buy button more eye-catching than the others. Guide their eyes to the decision you've already made for them.

Chapter 16: Price as a Positioning Tool

Raise the price to attract better customers.

The most toxic belief in business is that lowering prices makes you more competitive. The reality is that competing on price is a race to the bottom where the winner loses. In this chapter, you'll discover a counterintuitive truth, yet one supported by behavioral economics: price isn't just a collection mechanism; it's a positioning filter. Raising your rates is the fastest and most effective way to scare away troublesome customers and attract serious, committed, and action-ready buyers.

The myth of the customer "grateful" for the discount

There is a romantic narrative in sales that says: If I charge this customer a low price, he will be so grateful for the opportunity that he will be easy to work with, he will not cause any problems, and he will recommend me to others.

Anyone who has ever sold a professional service or a digital product knows that this is an absolute lie.

Due to a strange psychological anomaly, the exact opposite occurs. The customer who haggles over the last penny, the one who buys your book only because it was $0.99, or the company that hires you simply because you had the lowest bid, is invariably the customer who causes the most problems.

- They demand 24/7 attention.
- They question your methodology.
- They leave negative reviews for insignificant details.
- They never take responsibility for implementing what you sell them.

Why? Because when the price is low, the customer has no "skin in the game." They don't feel they've made a significant investment, so they don't respect your time, your product, or your authority.

The Psychology of the Premium Buyer

When you decide to raise your prices drastically, you leave the red ocean of budget options and enter the world of the premium buyer. This type of customer isn't looking to save money; they're looking to buy certainty, speed, and status.

By paying a high price, the premium buyer makes a psychological pact with himself: "I'm investing heavily in this, so I'm going to take it seriously."

Let's see how this rise in positioning completely changes the dynamics in three radically different business models:

1. In High Value Services (Example: Engineering and B2B)

Imagine you're applying to lead the oversight and supervision of a major road infrastructure project. The client needs guarantees that the pavement structure (with its exact thickness of granular base and asphalt) will be executed flawlessly.

If you offer the lowest fees, the corporate client doesn't think, "What a great saving." Their amygdala fires up and they think, "If they charge so little, they must be cutting staff, they lack experience, or they won't perform the topographic surveys with the necessary rigor."

In projects where the financial risk of failure is catastrophic, your high price signals to the client that their project will be secure. The premium buyer gladly pays a premium because they are purchasing risk mitigation.

2. In Physical Consumption Niches (Example: Sport Fishing)

The weekend angler who goes to the lake to hang out will look for the cheapest equipment at the store. But the competitive sport fisherman who seeks to catch large species (like a big catfish) operates under a different logic.

He knows that in the critical moment of tension, cheap line or substandard equipment will cost him the trophy. If you offer him an imported reel or a highly specialized, enticing formula at a premium price, he doesn't see it as an expense; he sees it as a performance tool. The high price positions your product as "the pros' gear." It appeals to the customer who doesn't argue, who values product technology, and who knows exactly what they're buying.

3. In Digital Publishing and Infoproducts (The KDP Ecosystem)

The effect of price as a filter is brutally visible in non-fiction books and technical manuals.

Let's say you publish a manual revealing the mathematical architecture behind casino systems, teaching how to master roulette or poker tables.

- If you sell it for $2.99, you'll attract curious people who will either skim through it and forget about it, or leave a bad review because "they didn't make millions on the first day."
- If you package that same content with a cinematic cover, optimize its metadata and indexing, and sell it for $19.99 or $24.99, the landscape changes. You attract serious players who will study the systems, apply mathematical probabilities at the tables, and value the information.

Furthermore, the math behind SEO here is undeniable: if your goal is to dominate international markets (France, Italy, Germany, Australia) and scale your monthly revenue to robust figures, you need to run Amazon Ads campaigns. If your royalties are $1 per sale, the cost per click (CPC) will leave you in the red on day one. A premium price gives you the necessary margins to crush your competition in the advertising bidding, buying the best keywords while they run out of budget.

How to perform the positioning jump

Raising your price isn't simply about changing a number on your dashboard and waiting for the money to roll in. It requires your entire brand infrastructure to scale up to support that new price without collapsing.

Here are the three operational pillars to raise your price and attract your ideal customer:

1. **The Visual Purge:**A premium price doesn't survive in cheap packaging. Before you even consider the price, make sure your visuals exude authority. For books, this means impeccably finished covers and meticulously designed interiors. For physical products or agencies, it means abandoning generic templates and investing in hyper-professional design.
2. **The Exclusion "Copy":**Start actively repelling bad customers in your product or service description. Use qualifying phrases.
   o *"This system is not for novices looking for easy money. It's designed for..."*
   o *"Our supervision is structured solely for infrastructure projects that require millimeter tolerances."*When you tell a cheap customer that this product "is not for him", you magnetically attract the high-level customer.
3. **Tactical Silence:**When you raise your prices, don't apologize or give lengthy justifications for your operating costs. Authority doesn't need justification. Present your proposal, demonstrate the transformative value, and then remain silent.

The opportunity cost of being cheap

Every day you keep your prices low for fear of losing sales, you're suffering a double penalty. First, you're working with suffocating margins that don't allow you to invest in key tools (like advanced analytics or international advertising). Second, and even more serious: you're filling your time and schedule with mediocre clients, which prevents you from having the space to serve the premium client when they finally arrive.

Your price is the gateway to your business. You decide how high you lock it and who has the right to enter.

Chapter 17: When and How to Raise Your Prices Without Losing Customers

The protocol for gradual increase with strategic communication.

The biggest obstacle to scaling your business's profitability isn't the market, the competition, or the algorithm; it's your own paralysis at the thought that if you raise prices, all your customers will flee. Here, you'll learn to defuse that psychological bomb. You'll discover that price increases aren't a risky event, but a predictable, mechanical protocol that, when communicated correctly, not only retains your best customers but also strengthens your authority.

The terror of mass exodus

There is a moment that paralyzes every product catalog owner, independent author, or technical consultant: the moment they realize that their margins are no longer sustainable.

Perhaps your advertising costs for penetrating international markets have increased. Perhaps the demands of your consulting projects require more attention. You know mathematically that you need to raise prices to reach your revenue targets, but fear is paralyzing you.

What if my readers stop buying my children's story series? What if construction companies look for a cheaper surveyor? What if my sales drop to zero and the algorithm buries me?

This fear stems from assuming that a customer's loyalty is solely based on your price tag. If you've applied the lessons from previous chapters (impeccable design, the halo effect, loss aversion, and authority positioning), your customer is loyal to the solution and the transformation, not to the pennies.

There are two completely different scenarios for implementing a price increase. One applies to large, automated catalogs; the other, to portfolios of recurring clients or high-value services. Let's look at the exact protocol for each.

Scenario 1: Physical Products, Books and E-commerce (The Silent Increase)

When you manage a catalog with dozens or hundreds of references (like a KDP book portfolio or a sport fishing tackle store), your advantage is that most of the traffic is made up of new customers every day.

You don't need to send out a press release to raise the price of a roulette strategy manual from $14.99 to $19.99. You simply raise it. The buyer who comes in tomorrow has no idea what it cost yesterday. Their anchor will be the new price.

However, to mitigate any algorithmic or conversion risk, use the Value-Added Ladder Protocol:

1. **Go up into the blind spot:**Increase the price by percentages that the brain doesn't register as aggressive (between 10% and 15%). A jump from $19.00 to $22.00 rarely stops a qualified buyer.
2. **Syncs with metadata enhancements:**Never raise the price while leaving the listing unchanged. Take this opportunity to update your long-tail keyword research for those specific markets (Italy, France, Germany, Australia). By improving SEO and adjusting your advertising campaigns, the product will reach a more qualified audience that won't question the new price.
3. **Renew the Halo Effect:**If you're going to double the price of a highly fermented fishing formula, change the label design or update the 3D images in the listing. If the packaging looks twice as professional, the brain immediately justifies the price increase.

By raising prices in your automated catalog, you'll have the profit margin you need to revitalize your ad campaigns (like Amazon Ads). You'll no longer be competing for cheap clicks; you'll be able to bid aggressively to dominate your niche.

Scenario 2: B2B Services and Recurring Customers (The Transition Protocol)

Raising your rates for a company that regularly hires you for technical oversight, design, or consulting requires a delicate touch. You can't be silent here. You must master the narrative.

The catastrophic mistake is sending a cold email that says: "Due to inflation and my operating costs, starting next month my rates will increase by 20%."

Your corporate client doesn't care about your operating costs. By arguing based on your own needs, you project weakness. The increase must be justified by the value they receive.

Execute the "Grandfathering" Protocol (Acquired Rights):

1. Freeze your best customers (Temporarily)

To your most valuable long-term and recurring clients, send a message informing them that the agency's or your services' rates have officially increased for the general public, but that, out of loyalty to their trust, their current prices will be frozen for the next 3 to 6 months.

- *The Neurological Effect:* The client doesn't feel attacked. They feel rewarded and protected. You've given them time to adjust their budgets, while reaffirming your high value in the international market.

2. The Update Message (The Perfect Copywriting)

When it comes time to apply the new rate to the existing base (or when you talk to an old customer who is returning after some time), the message should focus on the evolution of your capacity.

"Carlos, over the past year we've drastically optimized our data collection and on-site quality control processes. To continue guaranteeing this level of technical accuracy and exclusivity in our

reports, our structural rates have been updated to $X for this semester. I'd love for us to continue working together under this new standard."

No apologies. No lengthy explanations. Absolute firmness.

3. Say goodbye to energy vampires

Use price increases as a natural pruning tool. Those toxic clients who always demand discounts, pay late, or drain your technical and emotional energy are the first ones you should apply the maximum rate to without hesitation. If they accept it, their profitability will compensate for their behavior. If they leave, they've just freed up valuable space in your schedule for a premium client.

The Mathematics of Relief (The Irrational Fear of Abandonment)

Your amygdala will tell you: "If you raise the price by 20%, you will lose many customers."

Let's answer that with cold, hard numbers. Suppose you sell a consulting package for $1,000 and serve 10 clients per month. You bill $10,000. You decide to raise your rate by 25%, bringing it to $1,250.

Terrified, you watch as 2 of your clients decide not to renew (you lost 20% of your portfolio).

- **New situation:**You serve 8 clients at $1,250.
- **New billing:**$10,000.

What just happened? You're earning exactly the same amount of money, but you've recovered 20% of your free time. You have less operational workload, less stress, and more space available to prospect for new contracts at the updated rate.

Losing customers in the lowest price bracket is not a financial tragedy; it's a necessary operational optimization to scale your business towards solid goals.

Tactical Execution Summary

1. **New customers pay the new rate today:**Don't wait until January 1st. The next prospect who contacts you or the next product you list on the platform should have the updated price. Evaluate the actual market resistance, not what you imagine.
2. **Protect your allies:**Notify your existing customers well in advance (at least 60 days) that rates will undergo a structural update. Use the grace period to strengthen the relationship.
3. **Sell the upgrade, not the cost:**Eliminate words like "inflation," "costs," or "adjustments" from your business vocabulary. Replace them with "optimization," "new quality standard," and "greater responsiveness."
4. **Embrace the escape:**If a justified price increase, communicated elegantly and backed by undeniable visual authority, causes a percentage of your customers to leave, celebrate. Your business has just become leaner, more exclusive, and mathematically more profitable.

Chapter 18: Discounts that don't destroy your brand

The only three types of discounts that don't train your customers to expect deals.

Traditional discounts are the most addictive drug in e-commerce. They give you a quick sales boost today, but destroy your margins and your market position tomorrow. When you accustom the market to buying on sale, you're neurologically training your customers to never pay full price again. Here you'll discover how to use psychology to your advantage by applying the only three discount models that protect your catalog's authority and safeguard the profitability of your advertising campaigns.

The toxic cycle of "50% Off"

Imagine this scenario. You've just published a new edition of your advanced poker and roulette manual, or perhaps launched a premium fermented bait for sport fishing. The list price is $24.99.

Three days go by, sales are slow, and panic sets in. You log into your dashboard and slap a giant "50% off" sticker on it.

Immediately, some sales come in. You feel relieved. But what you don't see is the invisible, long-term damage you've just done to your brand.

1. **You destroyed your anchor of value:**The customer who bought it for $12.50 will never again believe your product is worth $25. Their brain has recalibrated the item's true value.
2. **You punished your best customers:**Those loyal customers who paid the full price on day one now feel cheated.
3. **You destroyed your acquisition margin:**If you were planning to use advertising to scale in international markets (such as France, Italy, or Germany), you've just wiped out the margin needed to win the bid for the most profitable keywords.

The market doesn't respect what's always on sale. If a brand is constantly being liquidated, the buyer assumes the quality is poor.

However, financial incentives are necessary to move volume or launch new products. The secret lies in how you frame the offer. An ethical and strategic discount is never perceived as an act of desperation; it's perceived as a privilege.

The 3 Secure Discount Models (Strategic Framework)

To inject liquidity or volume into your business without tarnishing your brand's Halo Effect, you must apply exclusively one of these three models:

1. The Stealth Discount (Incentive for Addition, Not Subtraction)

The worst mathematical mistake is cutting your base price. If a product costs $30 and you lower it to $20, you've lost $10 in net profit.

The Stealth Discount reverses the equation: instead of lowering the price, you temporarily increase the value by delivering bonuses that have a high perceived value but a low replication cost for you.

- **How to apply it:** You keep the price firm and unwavering at $30, but announce that, for a limited time, the purchase will include a complimentary product for free.
- **Example in action:** If you sell the children's series Magical Tales to Dream About, you don't offer a 20% discount on the physical book. Instead, you sell it at full price, but during the weekend you include a hidden link to download the audiobook (narrated with high-quality AI voices) at no extra cost.
- **The Neurological Effect:** The official book price is never compromised. The customer feels they've taken advantage of an incredible offer, but you haven't jeopardized your financial stability.
-

2. The Privilege Discount (The VIP Status)

A discount that's available to everyone on the store's homepage isn't a deal; it's simply your new low price. For a discount not to seem like a desperate offer, it should have some prerequisite for entry.

It should be a reward for past behavior, not a bribe for future behavior.

- **How to apply it:**You hide the discount from the general public. You only offer it to a highly qualified segment through a private channel (such as a mailing list of previous customers).
- **Example in action:**You're about to publish a new book on casino strategies. In the store, the product is released at its premium price of $29.99. But days before, you send an exclusive email to readers who purchased your previous books: "As a member of the Advanced Readers Circle, you have 48 hours to purchase the new edition at a 30% discount using this private link, before the catalog opens to the general public."
- **The Neurological Effect:**The customer doesn't feel the product is cheap; they feel special. The discount is perceived as recognition of their status, reinforcing brand loyalty.

3. The Momentum Discount (The Conditional Rapid Action)

International platform algorithms thrive on speed. A high sales volume within the first 72 hours can catapult your product to the first page of search results, drastically reducing your advertising costs.

To achieve that initial peak without permanently locking your price down, you use the Momentum Discount. This discount has one non-negotiable and irrevocable condition: it's tied to a time limit or absolute inventory.

- **How to apply it:**You launch the product at a lower price, but you communicate visually and in writing exactly when the price will rise and never go back down.

- **Example in action:**You've just formulated a new batch of your "La Bomba" bait to catch large cachama fish. In the description, you lay out the rules: "Special introductory price for the first 100 units. Once the 100th order is placed, the algorithm will automatically revert the price to its regular rate of $45. No exceptions."
- **The Neurological Effect:**You're using loss aversion to your advantage. The qualified buyer knows that if they hesitate, the penalty will be paying more tomorrow. When you actually cross the 100-unit mark and raise the price, you demonstrate to the market that your word is law. You've trained your customers to buy quickly on your next release.

The Iron Rule of Justification

There is a common thread in these three models that you should memorize: The human brain instinctively distrusts a low price that has no reason for being.

If you offer a discount without explaining why, the customer will assume the worst possible reason (it's poor quality, it's not selling, it's defective). To protect your market position, whenever you offer a financial advantage, you must verbalize the logical reason behind it.

- *Evil:*"Today only, 30% off!"
- *Good:*"To celebrate our entry into bookstores in Australia and Germany, we have released 50 digital copies at a 30% discount to fund our international launch campaign."

The first sentence triggers alarms in the amygdala. The second sentence provides the prefrontal cortex with a logical and transparent justification that defuses any suspicion.

Tactical Execution Summary

Before you touch your catalog's pricing settings again, apply this security filter:

1. **Kill generic discounts:**Eliminate "Mother's Day" or "Black Friday" discounts from your business strategy unless you use the Stealth Discount model (maintain price, add value).
2. **Protect the public front:**Your visible listing, cinematic-lit cover photos, and high-level description should always reflect your premium rate. Discounts are kept under wraps (in private emails, through hidden links, or in closed groups).
3. **Follow through on your threats:**If you offer a limited-time discount, you must restore the original price at midnight. If you give in and leave the discount "for a few more days," you've just lost your authority. The market will test you; make sure you don't blink.

Chapter 19: Price and Context: The same product is worth different things depending on where you sell it

The physical and digital environment as an amplifier or destroyer of value.

We naively believe that a product's value lies in its materials, the number of pages, or its software code. Behavioral economics demonstrates that 80% of perceived value comes not from the item itself, but from the environment where the customer encounters it. Here, you'll discover how the ecosystem surrounding your product—from optimizing your international listings to assessing customer risk—has the power to triple your price without you having to alter a single comma of your original product.

The $3 Million Subway Experiment

In January 2007, a man wearing a baseball cap entered a subway station in Washington, D.C. He stood against a wall, took a violin out of its case, and began to play for 45 minutes. He performed six of the most complex classical pieces ever written.

More than a thousand people passed by him. By the end, he had collected the disappointing sum of $32 in coins.

What the passersby didn't know was that the street musician was Joshua Bell, one of the world's finest violinists. The instrument he was holding was an original Stradivarius valued at $3.5 million. Just three days earlier, Bell had played the exact same repertoire at a Boston theater, where attendees paid more than $100 for a seat.

The product (the music) was mathematically identical. The quality of the performance was flawless. The talent was world-class. But in the context of a subway station with fluorescent lighting and dirty floors, the masterpiece was devalued to the status of $32 background noise.

The same thing happens in your business. It doesn't matter if you've developed the best mathematical system in the world or the most effective product on the market; if you sell it in the "subway station" of e-commerce, customers will pay you with coins.

The architecture of the digital concert hall

In mass commerce, the context is the screen. Every element surrounding the "Buy" button acts like the Boston theater or the dirty floor of the subway.

Imagine you publish a highly technical manual, for example, a book on probabilistic strategies for dominating the poker tables.

- **The "Subway" Context:**The listing appears with a generic cover image lacking cinematic lighting. The description contains dense blocks of text. Your keywords are so generic ("card games," "gambling") that the algorithm places you among two-dollar crossword puzzle magazines.
- **The Context "Theater":**The listing features rich content (A+). The homepage projects corporate luxury. You've used data intelligence tools (like Helium 10 or Jungle Scout) to identify the exact search intent. When the buyer lands there, the design and SEO practically shout, "You're in the right place. This is high-end."

In the first scenario, charging $25 seems like highway robbery. In the second, charging $25 seems like the standard entry price to join the ranks of professionals. The digital product is the same; the visual and metadata ecosystem dictated the price.

The International Context (Geography and Purchasing Power)

Context isn't just visual; it's also geographical. One of the biggest strategic mistakes product creators and publishers make is assuming that pricing is static across borders.

Launching a series of children's picture books or a technical manual requires understanding that the perceived value of money changes according to the buyer's postal code.

- A price of $9.99 may be the upper limit of friction in a Latin American market.
- That same product, translated and optimized for the markets of France, Italy, Germany or Australia, is inserted into economies with a purchasing power where $19.99 is considered an affordable entry ticket for a quality product.

If you have the ability to penetrate international markets through targeted advertising campaigns (Ads), exporting your product without adjusting the price accordingly is essentially throwing money away. The international algorithm rewards those who know how to charge in the local currency and understand the psychology of each territory.

The Context of Risk: Same Deliverable, Different Problem

In the sale of corporate services or specialized physical products, the context that triggers the price is called Customer Risk Level.

When the risk of failure is catastrophic for your buyer, the value of your solution multiplies, even if your work is exactly the same. Let's look at the stark difference in two distinct industries:

The Product/Service	Low Risk Context (Low Price)	High Risk Context (Premium Price)
Engineering / Surveying	A spreadsheet with leveling and topographic calculations for subdividing an empty rural lot is provided. A slight discrepancy will not have critical consequences.	**The exact same spreadsheet is delivered**But this time, it's for the technical oversight and supervision of a massive road infrastructure project. A millimeter error here costs millions in asphalt and legal penalties. The

The Product/Service	Low Risk Context (Low Price)	High Risk Context (Premium Price)
		document is worth 20 times that amount.
Sport Fishing	You sell a fermented bait formula in a neighborhood pet store to people who go fishing in the river on a Sunday afternoon to relax.	You're selling the same formula positioned at the entrance of a competitive tournament, where participants have invested thousands of dollars trying to catch a large fish (like a giant cachama) to win the grand prize. The competitive context drives up the price.
Conversion Optimization	You set up keyword campaigns for the listing of an amateur novel that generates $50 a month.	You configure the same backend prompt and keyword architecture for an international publishing catalog that already generates thousands of dollars and needs to dominate the European market.

The operational effort on your end barely changed. But the context of your client's problem transformed your solution from a "nice expense" into a "critical survival necessity."

The illusion of objectivity in e-commerce

You can't ask a customer to recognize the value of your product by isolating it from its context. The human brain doesn't work that way. Everything the buyer experiences in the second before seeing the price influences their financial assessment.

If you sell on your own web store, page load time, dark or elegant color palette, and typography are your Boston theater.

If you sell in ecosystems like Amazon KDP, your advertising campaigns, the accuracy of your SEO, and the cinematic quality of your covers are your Stradivarius.

If you compete on price, you're assuming your product is only worth what the general market dictates. If you elevate the context, you dictate to the market what it costs to enter your theater.

Tactical Execution Summary

1. **Audit of your subway station:**Review your weakest listings. Are your star products presented in an ecosystem that looks cheap? Identify if your keywords are attracting the wrong audience or if your images don't do the content justice.
2. **Identify High Risk:**Who is the buyer for whom your product isn't a luxury, but an operational or competitive necessity? Adapt your copywriting to speak exclusively to that customer who has a lot to lose if they don't buy from you.
3. **Price Location:**If you operate in multiple countries, don't just do simple currency conversions. Analyze the premium pricing ecosystem in Germany, Italy, or Australia, and adjust your branding to position yourself in the high-quality segment of each specific territory.
4. **Don't change the product, change the packaging:**Before spending months creating a new product to increase revenue, invest a week in improving the SEO, visual identity, and metadata of your existing product. The right context instantly multiplies your profit margin.

Chapter 20: How to Present the Price: Order Matters More Than Number

The exact sequence in which to reveal the price in a proposal.

We spend weeks debating whether to charge $99 or $120. However, in consumer psychology, the exact number is often less important than the timing of its disclosure. If the client sees the price before understanding the value, the number becomes a painful expense. If they see it after internalizing the transformation, it becomes a logical investment. Here, you'll learn to visually and verbally structure your B2B proposals and digital listings so that revealing your rate becomes the natural closing of a sale, not the beginning of a negotiation.

The "Last Page" mistake and the premature glance

There is a universal pattern in high-value corporate procurement. When you deliver a technical proposal to a client (for example, for the oversight of a road infrastructure project), what is the first thing the executive does upon receiving the PDF document or the physical folder?

He ignores the introduction, skips the methodology, doesn't read the topographic analyses or the structure of the granular base or the asphalt. He goes straight to the last page to find the total number.

Once your eyes catch that number, your brain sets a rigid anchor. Everything you read next (if you choose to read it at all) will be judged through the defensive lens of that number. Your brain won't be saying, "Wow, what a precise methodology"; it will be saying, "Does this methodology really justify the $15,000 I saw on the last page?"

The burden of proof shifts against you.

A similar dynamic occurs in e-commerce. If a user clicks on one of your ads in international markets (such as France or Germany) and lands on your page, their eyes will instinctively search for the price box before reading a single bullet point about your benefits.

To win the conversion game, you must design your offer or page to rigidly control the reading sequence. You must build the mountain of value before revealing the toll.

The B2B Framework: The Sandwich Sequence

When you sell premium services to companies, specialized consulting, or project management, you can't allow the client to skim the document at will. The price should never be isolated on a blank final page, because then it feels exposed and expensive.

The price should be sandwiched between Financial Impact and Immediate Execution. This is the exact sequence for an unbeatable proposal:

1. **Phase 1: The Diagnosis of Pain.**It starts with demonstrating that you understand the problem better than the client. (Example: "Currently, the lack of technical control is generating a risk of cost overruns of 15% in the foundation phase...").
2. **Phase 2: The Transformation Methodology.**How are you going to solve it? This includes your authority, control systems, and deliverables.
3. **Phase 3: The Financial Impact (The High Anchor).**Before the price, you remind the customer how much money you're going to save or generate for them. "Implementing this control will mitigate a risk valued at $120,000."
4. **Phase 4: The Investment (The Price).**Immediately after the impact, you present your rate. It is revealed as a small fraction of the previous number.
5. **Phase 5: The Next Immediate Step.**Don't end the document with a "Thank you." The customer's brain has just processed an expense; don't leave it silent. Continue the text on the same page with the startup instructions: "To ensure the start

of operations this Monday, the next step is to sign Attachment A..."

By surrounding the price with massive value above and tactical action below, the rate ceases to be a wall and becomes a simple stepping stone.

The Digital Sequence: Controlling the "Scroll" in E-Commerce

When selling physical products, digital tools, or publications on international platforms, the interface often forces you to display the price at the top. But you control the metadata, images, and rich content (A+).

The anatomy of a page that justifies high prices follows this strict visual order:

Order of Appearance	Element on Screen	Neurological Function
1. The Visual Impact (Hero)	Cover or main image with cinematic lighting and hyperrealistic quality.	**The Anchor of Authority.**Activate the Halo Effect. The brain instantly assumes the product is premium quality before even reading the price.
2. The Title and Subtitle	Keywords focused on pain and transformation (smart SEO).	**Qualification Filter.**If you're selling an advanced roulette or poker system, the title promises to master probability, justifying that it's not a cheap leisure text.

Order of Appearance	Element on Screen	Neurological Function
3. The Figure (The Price)	Clear presentation, preferably with a round or strategic format as seen in previous chapters.	**The Moment of Friction.**The brain evaluates the number against the weight of visual authority (Step 1 and 2).
4. Content A+ / Bullet Points	Interior graphics, mockups, success stories and the Cost of Inaction (COI).	**The Rider's Ammunition.**This is where the rational brain finds the technical arguments and social proof to justify the decision to add to cart.
5. Risk Reversal	Absolute guarantees visible before the final purchase button.	**Tonsil relaxation.**Elimination of the final fear of losing money.

The Principle of Immediate Contrast

There is a bias known as the Contrast Effect. The brain perceives differences more intensely when they are presented consecutively.

If you are going to present multiple pricing options (the three-level architecture of Chapter 15), the order in which the customer reads them alters your conversion rates.

Never present prices from lowest to highest.

If you present your $15 Basic package first, the brain gets stuck on that number. When it gets to the $120 Elite package, the amygdala screams that it's financial madness.

Always present from highest to lowest (Top-Down).

1. **Show the Elite Package first:**The customer sees the complete hardcover collection with audiobooks for $120. A high anchor is set. Their brain adjusts to that altitude.
2. **Show the second Premium Package:**The customer views the main set that solves their problem for $45.
3. **The Effect:**Coming from the $120 anchor price, the $45 package no longer feels like a forty-five dollar expense. It feels like a massive savings compared to the primary option.

Presenting the highest price first lubricates the acceptance of all subsequent rates.

The golden rule in sales calls

If you close B2B deals or sell services via video calls, the rule of order is inviolable: Whoever states the price and continues talking loses power.

When it comes time to reveal your fee after you have explained your diagnosis and methodology, say it with absolute clarity, without filler words, without nervous justifications, and do something that terrifies most salespeople: Be quiet.

- *"The investment to structure and implement the entire control system at the construction site is twelve thousand dollars."*
- *(Absolute silence).*

The silence following the price disclosure projects unwavering confidence. It demonstrates that the figure is a standard, not a starting point for bargaining. If you fill that silence with nervous explanations ("And well, this includes... and we can discuss payment options..."), you undermine the established positioning and signal to the client that your price is negotiable.

Tactical Execution Summary

1. **Restructure your PDFs and Presentations:**If you send proposals by email, make sure the price isn't left out on the last page. Place it between the Return on Investment (above) and the next operational steps (below).
2. **Apply the "Top-Down" method in your store:**Review your website and make sure that the most expensive options, complete bundles, and luxury editions are the first things that catch a customer's eye. Use these high prices as a protective shield for your mid-range flagship products.
3. **Own the silence:**If you sell in person or over the phone, record your next meeting. Analyze what you do in the five seconds after stating your price. If you try to justify it, you're sabotaging your own margins. State the number, trust the context you've built, and breathe.

Chapter 21: Anatomy of the objection "it's too expensive"

There are five different meanings behind that phrase. Learn to distinguish them.

The objection "it's too expensive" is, without a doubt, the most misunderstood phrase in the world of sales and e-commerce. When a customer utters or even thinks these words, your survival instinct screams at you to offer a discount. That's a fatal mistake. In consumer psychology, "expensive" rarely means "I don't have the money." Here you'll learn to decode the five hidden messages behind this objection and how to restructure your listings or proposals to neutralize each one before they ruin your sale.

The symptom, not the disease

Imagine you go to the doctor with a splitting headache and, without asking you any questions or checking your vital signs, the doctor decides to operate on your brain. That would be absolute negligence, because the headache is just a symptom; the cause could be stress, dehydration, or lack of sleep.

In corporate business and in the sale of digital products, the phrase "it's very expensive" is exactly the same: it's a superficial symptom.

If you react to that symptom by immediately lowering your price, you're essentially operating on the patient's brain when all they needed was a glass of water. You're crippling your profitability by failing to understand your customer's needs.

When a buyer stops in front of your B2B proposal or your online store listing and their brain concludes that "it's expensive," they are actually experiencing one of the following five cognitive short circuits.

Meaning 1: "I don't understand Return on Investment (ROI)"

The client has the budget, but you haven't shown them how your solution will give them back more money, time, or resources than they're currently providing. The number on the label looks like an expense, not an investment.

- **The B2B Scenario:** You're submitting a proposal for the oversight and supervision of a road infrastructure project. If the corporate client looks at your fees and says "it's expensive," it's because they think you're charging them just to "go and look at the construction site."
- **The Solution:** You need to quantify the disaster. Show them that the lack of precise, millimeter-level topographic control will cause them to waste material. Translate your work into their language: "If the leveling fails, they'll end up compensating for the error with the 9 cm of asphalt layer and the 30 cm of granular base. That's tens of thousands of dollars in cost overruns. My fee is insurance against that loss." Suddenly, your price stops being an expense and becomes a financial shield.

Meaning 2: "I'm comparing you to garbage" (The Anchor Problem)

The customer believes that your premium product is identical to the low-end options that flood the market, and doesn't understand why you charge three times as much as they do.

- **The E-Commerce Scenario:** You have a catalog of books published in international markets (France, Germany, Italy, Australia). You sell an advanced manual on mathematical systems and probability for poker and roulette tables for €19.99. The customer considers it "expensive" because Amazon's algorithm just showed them a generic €2.99 pamphlet written by artificial intelligence and lacking any mathematical rigor.

- **The Solution:**Your product suffers from visual commoditization. If your item looks the same as the $2.99 one, the customer will never pay $19.99. You must differentiate yourself from the rest using the Halo Effect. Your cover design, the strategic use of keywords in your listing, and your rich content must all exude authority. When you project absolute exclusivity, the buyer stops comparing you to the cheaper product.

Meaning 3: "I don't trust you to give me the result" (Perceived Risk)

The customer desperately wants the result and has the money in their pocket, but their amygdala is paralyzed by the fear of making a mistake, being scammed, or looking like a fool if the product fails.

- **The Niche Scenario:**A sport fisherman is about to buy your fermented bait formula ("the bomb") at a premium price. His goal is to catch a heavyweight cachama in a tournament this weekend. When he hesitates in front of your shopping cart and thinks, "It's expensive," it's not because of the money; it's because in the past he's bought baits that promised him the world and sent him home empty-handed.
- **The Solution:**Risk reversal and destructive social proof. They need to see real testimonials, photos of high-quality catches achieved with your formula, and an unwavering performance guarantee. You have to absorb their operational fear. If you eliminate risk, price ceases to matter.

Meaning 4: "The problem doesn't hurt me enough... yet" (Cost of Inaction)

The customer acknowledges that you have a good product, but doesn't feel any urgency. They're in their comfort zone.

- **The Consumption Scenario:**A father sees your collection of illustrated children's stories and, although he loves the premise of "Magical Tales to Dream," decides that $25 is too much for a book and closes the tab.

- **The Solution:**You're selling features ("a beautifully illustrated storybook") instead of selling the antidote to bleeding. You need to reactivate Loss Aversion in your comics. If you remind them of the frustration of nightly battles, the stress of not having time for themselves at the end of the day, and the loss of their own sleep, the $25 becomes a minimal investment in exchange for peace of mind and guaranteed rest.

Meaning 5: "I really don't have the money" (The Wrong Customer)

This is the only time the objection is literal. The prospect simply doesn't have the purchasing power to pay for your product or service.

- **The Setting:**Someone clicked on your international ad campaign out of curiosity, but their monthly budget doesn't allow them to pay a high price.
- **The Solution:**You do nothing. You don't lower your price, you don't offer a compassionate discount, and you don't adapt your business model. You acknowledge the interest and let it go. Lowering your standards to accommodate those who can't afford you is the fastest way to destroy your brand and exhaust your operational energy.

Tactical Framework: The Isolation Question

If you're selling face-to-face or via video call and you hear the phrase "it's too expensive," you must remain calm, maintain eye contact, and use the most powerful tool in closing sales: Isolation.

Respond in a genuinely curious and relaxed tone:

"I understand perfectly, Carlos. And just out of curiosity, to make sure we're on the same page... when you say the proposal is expensive, what exactly are you comparing it to?"

That simple question breaks the automatic response in his brain.

- If they respond with the price of your cheap competitor, you are facing Meaning 2. You explain again the massive difference in your technical quality.
- If they answer "I don't know if I'll recover the investment", you're facing Meaning 1 or 3. You go back to the board and mathematically illustrate their savings and your guarantees.
- If they reply "we simply don't have that money in the account", you are facing Meaning 5. You say goodbye politely.

In e-commerce (Amazon, your own stores, Shopify), you can't ask this question live, so your product pages must proactively address objections 1, 2, 3, and 4 in the text, before the customer even sees the buy button.

The high price is never the real problem. The problem is the absence of a value context to support it.

Chapter 22: Language that Increases Perceived Value

Words and phrases that activate the buyer's reward system.

The cinematic design of your covers and the mathematical structure of your pricing are useless if the words that accompany them sound cheap. The human brain unconsciously assigns a monetary value to certain words; some trigger fear and friction, while others release dopamine and a sense of authority. Here you'll discover how to conduct a linguistic audit of your catalog and your proposals, replacing the "language of spending" with the "language of premium transformation."

The invisible alchemy of words in commerce

Imagine you're writing the final report for the technical oversight of a massive road infrastructure project. If you present the document stating that the structure has "a good layer of asphalt and large stones underneath," the corporate client will panic and doubt your professionalism. But if you describe the precise technical rigor of the structure: "9 cm of asphalt layer supported by 30 cm of granular base and 30 cm of crushed stone," the perception of control and safety is absolute. The physical work was the same, but the technical language justified the authority.

In e-commerce, in the sale of information products, and in digital publishing, the exact same neuro-linguistic rule applies.

Mediocre salespeople write product descriptions; high-value strategists write perception architecture. Every bullet point in your listing, every subheading you optimize with tools like Helium 10 or Jungle Scout, and every call to action should be calibrated to trigger the customer's reward system.

When a buyer reads your page, they're not just scanning keywords for international SEO; they're looking for linguistic signals that confirm they're about to make the right decision.

The Precision Bias (The Authority of the Specific)

The human brain is naturally wary of generic, roundabout adjectives. Words like "a lot," "fast," "excellent quality," or "great design" have been so overused by cheap marketing that they've lost all their meaning. Today, they're just noise.

The fastest way to increase the perceived value of your product is to replace generic language with hyper-specific language.

- **In the fiction publication:**Don't say, "A very pretty picture book for children." Say, "Volume One of Magical Tales to Dream About, designed with high-contrast illustrations and narrative schemes that reduce resistance to nighttime sleep."
- **In sports niches:**If you're selling a bait formula, don't say "Attracts lots of fish." Say: "Fast-fermenting formula, specifically designed to ensure catches of large species like cachama in tournament environments."

Technical precision acts as a sedative for the amygdala (the fear center). When the customer reads exact specifications, they automatically assume that the product's creator is an absolute expert in the field.

Transformation Verbs vs. Static Nouns

A classic mistake when writing descriptions on mass publishing platforms is to list features (nouns) instead of selling the action (verbs).

The client doesn't buy "pages," "software," "formulas," or "matrices." They buy the final result. You must use active verbs that give them control of the situation.

Observe the change in hierarchy when you apply transformation verbs to a casino strategy manual:

- *Noun Language (Cheap):*"A book about roulette and poker with mathematical systems and probability."
- *Verb Language (Premium):*"Dominate the poker tables. Protect yourself against the house edge and implement mathematical probability systems that multiply your profitability in roulette."

The verbs "dominate," "shield," "execute," and "multiply" activate dopamine. They make the reader visualize themselves taking action and winning.

The Dictionary of Authority: Translation of Terms

To charge more, you must eliminate mediocre vocabulary from your sales pages, emails, and proposals. Here's a neurological translation chart to audit your texts immediately:

The Language of Spending (Eliminate It)	The Language of Investment (Use it)	The Psychological Effect
Price / Cost	Investment / Professional Fee	"Price" hurts. "Investment" suggests a future financial or emotional return.
Expense / Pay	Secure / Access / Book	"Paying" activates the pain center. "Securing" activates the instinct of possession and security.
Discount / Sale	Privilege / Launch Advantage	"Discount" devalues your brand. "Privilege"

The Language of Spending (Eliminate It)	The Language of Investment (Use it)	The Psychological Effect
		elevates the buyer's status.
Cheap / Economical	Efficient / Highly Profitable	"Cheap" is for novices. "Profitability" is the language of decision-makers.
Made with AI / AI Illustrations	Architectural Prompt Design / Cinematic Rendered Lighting	It emphasizes the dominance of the tool (human talent) over the generic machine.
I'm going to help you...	We are going to implement/execute...	"Helping" sounds like charitable giving. "Implementing" sounds like corporate methodology and process engineering.

The language of the "Cost of Inaction" (Justified fear)

As we saw in the chapters on Loss Aversion, the most persuasive language isn't always positive. When you raise the price of a service or a technical manual, you should use phrases that highlight the hidden losses the customer will incur if they choose to ignore your offer.

Loss anchor phrases:

- *"Every day you publish without optimizing your metadata in the backend, you are giving away your share of the European market to lower-quality competitors."*
- *"Sitting at a high-blind table without mastering these variables is equivalent to betting blind."*

This type of language isn't aggressive; it's clinical. You're diagnosing a condition the client has, mentally preparing them to pay for the treatment (your product) with complete gratitude.

Closing Exercise: The Linguistic Purge

Open the listing of your most profitable product, or the last business proposal you sent, and apply the 3 C's rule:

1. **Adjective hunt:**Find and eliminate words like "good," "amazing," "fast," or "easy." Replace them with data, millimeter tolerances, precise metrics, or quantifiable benefits.
2. **Verb change:**Review the bullet points on your Amazon product page or your website. If they begin with an article or a noun, rewrite them to start with a transformation verb in the imperative mood (Master, Ensure, Optimize, Avoid).
3. **Status audit:**Read the text aloud. If the tone sounds like you're "begging" for the purchase, delete it. Rewrite it imagining you're the undisputed leader in your industry. Authority isn't asked for; it's assumed from the very first line.

Chapter 23: How to respond to the client's comparative Excel spreadsheet

The exact protocol for when you are compared to the cheapest competitor.

It's the most dreaded moment in corporate negotiations and online sales: the client pulls out a spreadsheet, places you side-by-side with your cheapest competitor, and asks you to "justify" why you charge twice as much if, seemingly, they offer the same thing. Here you'll discover why trying to win that mathematical argument is a death trap, and you'll learn the psychological protocol to destroy that Excel spreadsheet, changing the rules of the game so that the higher price is the only logical option.

The "Characteristics Table" Trap

Imagine you're in a meeting to close an important contract. The corporate client projects an Excel file. Column A lists your services. Column B lists the services of a competitor. Both promise to deliver the same project, but the competitor's final number is 40% lower than yours.

The customer looks at you and asks the trick question: "Your competition offers me the same thing for much less. Can you match the price?"

The natural instinct of most salespeople is to panic and start defending themselves line by line: "Well, my team is better, we're faster, I have more experience...".

You just lost the sale.

The moment you start defending your features against those of a cheaper option, you have validated the customer's premise: you have accepted that you and the cheap competitor are "pears to pears" and that the only real difference is the cost.

The reality your client is unaware of (and which it's your job to illuminate) is that comparative Excel spreadsheets are an illusion. Spreadsheets only measure operational effort and physical deliverables, but they never measure risk, the cost of failure, or the level of mastery.

The B2B Protocol: Destroying Excel in High-Value Services

When you sell consulting, design, or corporate services where a mistake costs a fortune, you can't allow yourself to be evaluated like a supermarket product. You must apply the Venture Investment Protocol.

Let's say you're competing for the technical supervision and oversight of a road infrastructure project. The client compares your proposal with that of a surveyor or engineer who charges half as much.

Don't talk about your resume. Talk about the catastrophe the client's Excel spreadsheet is omitting.

The exact answer (The Authority Script):

"I completely understand why your analyst put both proposals in the same table because, on paper, we'll both be submitting spreadsheets and topographic reports. But I have a question regarding structural risk: This project requires millimeter tolerances in a structure with 9 cm of asphalt, 30 cm of granular base, and 30 cm of crushed stone. If the supplier for column B makes a calculation error due to a lack of rigor in the field, who bears the cost of demolishing and rebuilding the damaged sections? Them, or you? My fee isn't for delivering a paper report; my fee is the insurance that protects the profitability of your project against catastrophic cost overruns. We're not competing in the same category as column B."

The Neurological Effect: You've taken the client out of the "savings" mindset and thrust them headfirst into the "survival" mindset. The spreadsheet becomes completely useless because they've just realized that comparing a premium auditor to a cheap provider based solely on price is a suicidal risk for their company.

The E-Commerce Protocol: The Silent Comparison

In the sale of digital products, physical books in international markets, or sporting goods, the comparative spreadsheet doesn't happen in a boardroom. It happens silently in the buyer's mind while they have two browser tabs open.

Imagine a customer in the Italian or French market looking for a book to master the mathematics of roulette. On one tab, they see your advanced strategies manual for €19.99. On another tab, they see a generic brochure on card games for €2.99. Or, in another niche, a sport fisherman compares your high-performance fermented dough formula for $30 with a basic dough for $5 in an online store.

If your listing only lists features (number of pages, grams of product), the customer will choose the cheaper option. To eliminate this silent comparison, you must inject Identity Differentiators directly into your bullet points and descriptions.

You have to write your listing assuming that the customer is looking at the cheap competition at that exact moment.

The Automatic Text Disqualification Framework:

- **Attacking the competitor's weakness (without naming them):**"Unlike the inexpensive options on the market that dissolve in water in minutes, this formula is designed with a heavy fermentation grade that resists currents to attract only tournament species."
- **Audience positioning:**"This is not a motivational book or a pamphlet of basic advice. It is a pure statistical system structured for players who treat the casino as an investment, not a pastime."

When you do this, you take away the customer's ability to compare you. You're telling them, "That cheap product you're looking at is for beginners. If you're a professional, this is the only product that will work for you."

The 3 iron rules in the face of price pressure

If the customer continues to pressure you to lower the price or match the competitor's rate, you must maintain your positioning by applying these three rules:

1. **Never cut the price without cutting the deliverable:**If you give in and lower your price by 30% while keeping the service the same, the client will think, "They were trying to rip me off from the start." If your client says, "I only have the competitor's quote," your response should be, "Perfect. To reach that number, we'll eliminate the quick response guarantee, remove the weekly reports, and remove the SEO optimization from the proposal. That way, we can fit it into that price." Almost always, the client prefers to pay the full price to avoid losing out on the benefits.
2. **Don't speak ill of the competition; explain their business model:**Don't say, "Competitor X does terrible work." Say, "That agency's business model is based on massive volume with junior staff. That's fine if you're looking for something quick and generic. Our model is handcrafted, in-depth, and based on precise data. It depends on the level of execution your project needs today."
3. **Maintain a willingness to walk away:**Absolute negotiating power belongs to the party who least needs the agreement. If the company insists on treating you like a generic B-column employee, you should be prepared to politely close your folder, wish them well, and leave the table. That show of authority often gets you called back before you even leave the building.

Tactical Execution Summary

1. **Change the focus of the conversation:**If you're compared on operating price, you're responsible for the financial risk. Force the client to calculate the "Cost of Inaction," or the cost of the cheaper provider making a serious mistake.
2. **Use the "Yes, but...":**When a competitor shows you a lower price, accept it calmly. "It's true, their price is very attractive. But our specialty isn't competing on cost, but rather on eliminating risk. What level of error tolerance does your project have at this time?"
3. **Isolate your products in e-commerce:**In your international Amazon listings, protect your price by increasing the Halo Effect. If your cover image is cinematic and your description filters out newcomers, the algorithm will stop matching you with cheap, two-dollar options, naturally setting you apart in the consumer's mind.

Chapter 24: Negotiating without giving in: the art of reverse anchoring

Negotiation techniques based on cognitive psychology, not cunning.

Traditional negotiation teaches you to be a "shark," to use pressure tactics, and to play a tiring game of tug-of-war where both parties end up frustrated. Behavioral economics offers a much more elegant and profitable path. Here you'll discover how to use Reverse Anchoring, a psychological technique that allows you to defend your higher rates without having to argue, by getting the client to convince their own brain that asking for a discount is a bad idea.

The instinct to concede (Why we lose before we even speak)

When a potential client tells you, "I love your proposal, but it's out of my budget," your reptilian brain goes into panic. The fear of losing the sale triggers a conditioned reflex: immediate concession.

You nervously start offering discounts, proposing payment plans, or giving away additional bonuses.

What happens in the buyer's mind when you do this? Their amygdala (the threat radar) goes into overdrive. They think, "If they were willing to lower their price by 20% so quickly, it means their original price was fake. They were trying to overcharge me." By giving in without a strategy, you don't save the sale; you destroy trust.

To negotiate in the high-value ecosystem, you must abandon bargaining tactics and enter the realm of cognitive architecture. The goal is not to win an argument, but to shift the client's frame of reference.

The Psychology of Reverse Anchoring

Reverse anchoring is not about defending your price, but about attacking the cost of the alternative.

In a standard negotiation, the client tries to anchor the conversation downwards, focusing on their own budget or what your cheapest competitor charges. Your job is to apply reverse anchoring: to violently shift the attention upwards, focusing the conversation on the cost of failure.

Let's see how this psychology is applied in three different scenarios:

Scenario 1: B2B Negotiation and High Responsibility Projects

Imagine you're negotiating fees for the technical supervision and oversight of a road infrastructure project. The corporate client asks you to adjust your budget to match that of a less experienced engineer.

If you negotiate from a position of weakness, you'll say, "I can lower the price by 10% if we close today." If you apply Reverse Anchoring, you'll say:

"I understand the budget constraint. However, my focus here isn't on my fee, but on your risk. A structure requiring 9 cm of asphalt and 30 cm of granular base doesn't forgive topographic or leveling errors at the work sites. If we agree to reduce the scope of supervision to fit that budget, the risk of premature structural failure increases. Repairing that failure will cost you ten times my fee. My price is non-negotiable because the security of your investment should be too."

The customer stops thinking about saving a few dollars and starts thinking about the terror of a million-dollar overcharge. The anchor has been inverted.

Scenario 2: Niche E-commerce (The Silent Anchor)

When selling physical products or specialized formulas, you can't talk to the customer. The negotiation happens on the sales page.

If you sell hyper-fermented bait ("the bomb") for sport fishing of heavy species like cachama, your price of $35 may seem high compared to generic lures at $5. The customer tries to negotiate mentally: "I'd rather buy the cheap one."

Reverse anchoring in your copywriting should remind you of the value of the entire ecosystem:

"You've spent $100 on fuel, $50 on entry to the specialty lake, and you have top-of-the-line equipment. Are you going to risk the tournament trophy to save $30 on the most important link between you and the fish?"

The anchor is no longer the $35 of the product; the anchor is the $150 and the time that the fisherman has already invested and does not want to waste.

Scenario 3: Negotiating Information Products and Software

You sell a mathematical system for mastering probability at casino tables (roulette or poker). You offer it for $49.99 in international markets (France, Germany, Italy). A user writes to you or thinks that a book shouldn't cost that much.

Reverse Anchoring redirects attention to the actual battlefield:

"You're not buying paper and ink. You're buying a loss prevention system. $49.99 is less than what the casino will take from you in the first five minutes if you sit down at the table without mastering these statistical variables."

The Rule of Asymmetric Concession (If you take away money, you take away blood)

Sometimes, the client genuinely doesn't have the budget, and you need to close the deal. The golden rule of behavioral economics for these situations is Asymmetric Concession.

Never, under any circumstances, lower your price while maintaining the same level of service or product. If the customer wants to pay less, the offer must be visibly reduced.

- **The Client says:**"We only have $8,000 approved for the audit; we can't pay the $10,000."
- **The Strategic Response:**"I understand. We can adjust the proposal to $8,000. To achieve this, we will remove the weekly on-site monitoring visits and the optimization reports from the second phase, delivering only the basic technical document. Shall we proceed with this reduced version?"

This triggers loss aversion. Seeing that you're taking away valuable parts of the service to fit their budget, 80% of corporate clients magically find the original quote. They want the full package. If they ultimately accept the reduced version, you've protected your profit margin per hour worked and maintained your authority.

The Power of the Tactical "No"

The best negotiator is not the one with the most persuasive words; it is the one with the least emotional need to close the deal.

The consumer's brain is accustomed to desperate salespeople who say yes to everything. When you encounter a difficult prospect demanding the world at half price, delivering a polite but firm "No" creates a cognitive shock.

"Unfortunately, given the level of technical precision we employ, we cannot absorb that discount without compromising the quality of the

result. It seems we are not the right supplier for this stage of your project. I wish you every success."

By taking the offer off the table, you reverse the power dynamic. Your brand's halo effect skyrockets. The client perceives that if you're willing to part with money, it's because your schedule is full and your product is as good as you claim. Often, this tactical "no" is precisely what makes the client return the next day, accepting your original terms.

Tactical Execution Summary

1. **Change the anchor focus:**Before your next sales meeting or before you publish your product page, clearly state the catastrophic cost of not hiring you. That's your reverse anchoring weapon.
2. **Prepare your menu of cuts:**If you're going to negotiate a B2B contract, go into the meeting knowing exactly which elements of your service you're going to cut if the client demands a lower price. The concession should hurt them, not your profit margin.
3. **Become desensitized to silence:**After presenting your reverse anchoring argument or refusing an unreasonable discount, remain completely silent. Let the client grapple with their own cognitive dissonance. Whoever breaks the silence to justify themselves loses the negotiation.

Chapter 25: Silence, pause and presence: the psychology of timing

What you do after stating the price determines whether they accept it or negotiate.

Most sales aren't lost because of the product or the price, but because of the anxiety of the person presenting it. There's an unwritten rule in behavioral economics: whoever speaks first after mentioning the price loses. Here you'll learn to master the most uncomfortable yet most profitable tool in closing sales: silence. You'll discover how to use tactical timing in both corporate meetings and the visual architecture of your e-commerce listings.

The rushed fishing line syndrome

In sport fishing for large species like cachama, there's one unbreakable rule once you cast a specialized bait into the water: you must give the fish time to take it firmly. If you succumb to anxiety, let the adrenaline get the better of you, and pull on the line at the first sudden movement of the water, all you'll achieve is dislodging the hook from its mouth and losing the catch.

In high-value negotiations and sales, the exact same phenomenon occurs. Price is your moment of tension.

The most common rookie mistake (and the one that wastes the most money) is the "nervous justification." The professional presents their proposal, reveals a high fee, and, feeling the weight of that number hanging in the air, panics at the client's silence. To fill that void, they start talking again:

- *"...but of course, we can review the payment methods."*
- *"...and well, if you think it's too high, we can remove some things."*
- *"...but remember that this includes technical support."*
-

You just ruined the closing.

By speaking immediately after giving the price, you send your customer's amygdala a neurological signal of insecurity. Your own body language and words have just told them, "I think this price is too high myself, please don't be upset." You've just given them permission to haggle.

The Neuroscience of Tactical Silence

When you reveal a significant price, your client's brain enters a state of deep processing. Their prefrontal cortex is calculating the risk, comparing your figure against the "Cost of Inaction" (the pain of not buying), and visualizing the end result.

This process consumes energy and takes time. The client's silence is not a rejection; it's a mathematical calculation.

If you disrupt that calculation with your nervousness, you reset their cognitive process and introduce doubt where there was none. Your job, at the exact moment you reveal your price, is to establish an unshakeable presence.

Let's see how this silence plays out in the two major sales ecosystems:

1. Timing in B2B Services and Consulting (The Face-to-Face)

Imagine you're in a construction company's boardroom presenting a proposal for the technical supervision and oversight of a massive road infrastructure project. You've already established your technical authority, detailing how your control will ensure that the exact structure (9 cm of asphalt, 30 cm of granular base, and 30 cm of crushed stone) is executed without catastrophic tolerances.

The final slide arrives. This is the script for perfect execution:

1. **State the number in a flat voice (midnight announcer's voice):**Don't raise your voice at the end of the sentence as if you were asking a question. Say it as if you were telling the time. "To ensure the successful completion of this project, our investment in project oversight is twenty-five thousand dollars."
2. **Close your mouth and hold your gaze:**Don't smile too much, don't look at your notes. Look your interlocutor in the eye with complete composure.
3. **Withstands pressure:**The silence may last 5, 10, or even 30 seconds. It will seem like an eternity. You will feel a biological urge to speak. Don't.

Whoever breaks this silence assumes a position of weakness at the table. When the corporate client finally speaks, 80% of the time they'll say, "Okay, when do we start?" or "Good, send the contract to the purchasing department." If they question the price, apply the Reverse Anchoring technique we learned in the previous chapter. But never speak first.

2. Visual Timing in E-Commerce and Digital Catalogs

If you have an automated business model or manage an international catalog on KDP, you're not in front of the customer to be silent. However, in digital commerce, silence translates into White Space (Visual Timing).

The human brain needs visual "breathing" before and after processing a price tag. If your store or listing shoves the price into a dense block of text, flashing timers, and garishly colored buttons, the customer feels overwhelmed.

- **Application in high-level niches (e.g., Systems and Strategy):**If you publish a sophisticated mathematical manual for mastering roulette and poker in markets like Germany, Italy, or France, the price shouldn't compete with the text. Separate the price. Use premium content to create a minimalist design where the price stands alone, surrounded by white space. That visual space conveys the same authority as silence in a boardroom. It means: "We're not in a hurry. We know what this is worth."

- **Application in narrative and collections (e.g., children's books):**If you're offering the complete Magical Dream Stories collection in a $45 premium package, let the box art and the value proposition rest on the screen. Don't pop up with "10% off if you buy now" the moment the user's mouse hovers over the price. Allow the parent to process the emotional value of the purchase (peaceful nights) rather than the price, without interrupting their cognitive process with cheap stimuli.

The Power of Presence (The Energy of the Expert)

Silence only works if it's backed by presence. Presence is the inner conviction that even if this customer doesn't buy from you, your business will continue to grow exactly the same, because out there are hundreds of customers who do value your quality.

Clients have an incredibly accurate radar for desperation. If you need the money to pay the office rent next week, your body language (or the aggressiveness of your follow-up emails) will give you away.

To maintain the silence, you must convince yourself of an undeniable reality of business: You are the prize.

The client has the money, but money is an abundant resource that is printed every day. You have the knowledge, the infrastructure, the process architecture, and the system that solves their problem. The solution is the scarce resource. When you internalize that you are making an exchange where they gain more than they spend, silence ceases to be awkward and becomes a simple stance of professional dignity.

Tactical Execution Summary

1. **Train silence:**In your next sales conversation, no matter how small, practice stating your rate and then remaining completely silent. Mentally count to ten. Observe how the client takes the lead and responds. It's a muscle; you need to train it.
2. **Audit the visual noise:**Open your listings on mobile devices. When the user scrolls and reaches the price area, does the design feel overwhelming or clean? Remove anything that screams desperation around the buy button. Give the price space.
3. **Forbid yourself the word "but":**After stating a price, the word "but" is poison. Erase phrases like "It's $5,000, but we can work around it" from your email templates and your business vocabulary. Authority has the final say. The client decides whether to walk through the door or not.

Chapter 26: Your 30-Day Pricing Plan

Week-by-week roadmap to redesign your entire pricing structure.

Reading about behavioral economics and cognitive biases is fascinating, but theory without execution is just entertainment. It's time to take action. This chapter is your tactical trench manual. Here, we'll consolidate all the strategies from the previous chapters into a 30-day action plan, designed step-by-step to purge your catalog, structure your offerings, and raise your rates without disrupting your cash flow or paralyzing your operations.

The bridge between theory and billing

Changing a business's pricing structure, especially when managing a complex ecosystem with over 200 published titles or handling high-responsibility technical projects, can be daunting. The most common mistake is trying to change everything in a single afternoon, creating visual and operational inconsistencies.

Repositioning requires surgical patience. This four-week roadmap divides the process into four separate phases: Visual Audit, Offer Architecture, Metadata Refinement, and Financial Launch.

Your ultimate goal by the end of Day 30 is to have a pricing ecosystem that works for you, attracting qualified customers and bringing you mathematically closer to your monthly revenue scalability goals.

Week 1: Halo Effect Audit and Visual Positioning (Days 1 to 7)

You can't charge premium rates if the storefront reeks of mediocrity. This week, no one's touching the prices; the sole objective is to protect the perceived quality so that, when the price goes up, the customer's brain instantly justifies it.

- **Day 1-2: Hunting for weak pixels.**Review your product covers and service presentations. If you publish technical manuals or literature, be sure to use advanced prompt engineering to generate images with cinematic lighting and hyper-realistic finishes. If you present B2B proposals, eliminate any generic templates.
- **Day 3-4: Cleaning the concert hall.**Apply the "theater auditorium" approach. Review the rich content (A+) of your listings. A specialized product for mastering probability in casinos or a tournament bait like "the bomb" for cachama fishing cannot have a plain text block description. Structure the text with bolding and a clear hierarchy.
- **Day 5-7: Audit of Authority Language.**Review the bullet points and descriptions. Replace static nouns with verbs of transformation. If you're presenting a project management methodology, eliminate weak phrases and assert control: "Strict supervision of road structure: 9 cm of asphalt, 30 cm of granular base, and 30 cm of crushed stone, guaranteeing millimeter tolerances in the field." Technical language numbs the fear of the price.

Week 2: Offer Architecture and Packaging (Days 8 to 14)

This week you will transform your catalog of isolated products into logical conversion traps using the rule of three and the Decoy Effect.

- **Day 8-9: Definition of the "Hero" (The Premium Level).**Choose your product or service with the best margin and highest success rate. This will be your Level 2. Its price should be anchored in Value (Return on Investment) and not in Cost.
- **Day 10-11: Creation of the Luxury Anchor (The Elite Level).**Design a significantly more expensive version of your core offering to protect the price of your Premium Tier. If you manage the Magical Tales to Dream series, your Elite Tier could be a hardcover edition that includes immersive audiobooks narrated with AI-powered speech synthesis technology (like Eleven Labs). Seeing that exclusive bundle

makes the price of the traditional book psychologically irresistible.

- **Day 12-14: Assembling the "Cost of Inaction" (COI).**For each premium package you've just created, write an introductory paragraph that quantifies what the customer is currently missing out on. Transform the "not buying" option into an unacceptable scenario.

Week 3: Ecosystem Optimization and International SEO (Days 15 to 21)

Showing the right price to the wrong customer will still seem expensive. This week, we'll align your new structure with the right qualified traffic and purchasing power.

- **Day 15-17: In-depth Keyword Research.**Use data intelligence tools (Helium 10, Jungle Scout, or B2B software) to scan high-value search intent. A buyer searching for "gambling" is looking for deals; a buyer searching for "statistical systems roulette poker" is willing to pay for high-level technical education.
- **Day 18-20: Backend and International Localization.**Prices aren't universal. Adjust indexing and hidden metadata to position your product in the highest-spending markets (France, Italy, Germany, the Netherlands, and Australia). Ensure that the keywords in each language reflect a premium purchase intent.
- **Day 21: Risk Reversal.**Draft and prominently display the guarantees for your services or products. Before moving to the final stage, the customer should feel that the full responsibility for any potential failure rests on your shoulders, not their wallet.

Week 4: Silent Launch and Scalability (Days 22 to 30)

It's time to update price tags and open the traffic tap to validate the new financial ecosystem.

- **Day 22-23: The Official Increase.**In automated ecosystems (like Amazon KDP or online stores), apply the price increase directly. Remove the ".99" if your goal is pure corporate prestige, or keep it if the product falls into the niche impulse-buy category.
- **Day 24-26: Advertising Reconfiguration (Amazon Ads and PPC).**With your new profit margin established, your cost-per-click (CPC) limit has just expanded. Set up aggressive advertising campaigns targeting your key international markets. Now that your product projects a massive halo effect and a premium price, you can crush the cheap competition in advertising bids without going into the red.
- **Day 27-29: Monitoring and Tactical Silence.**The first sales will come in. Don't panic if the overall conversion rate drops slightly; remember that you now need fewer sales to generate the same or higher revenue. If you have existing corporate clients, implement the transition protocol and temporarily freeze their rates.
- **Day 30: System Consolidation.**Review the numbers. With improved royalty margins and profitable ad campaigns running in international markets, the vehicle is ready to accelerate. The goal of scaling revenue to solid levels (like the $1,000 monthly mark in automated royalties) is now a simple matter of maintaining SEO optimization and letting the pricing architecture do its job.

Your Next Move

You've reached the end of the theoretical design and the execution timeline. The pricing architecture you have in your hands isn't about deceiving the consumer; it's about making it easier for their brain to recognize the true and profound value of what you offer.

Implement Day 1 today. Audit your most important image and start building your empire from visual perception. The market will pay the standard you have the courage to set.

Chapter 27: How to test prices without risking your business

A/B testing methodology applied to prices in services and physical products.

Changing a price that's already generating sales feels like trying to defuse a bomb: the fear of cutting the wrong wire and destroying your conversions paralyzes you. However, the only way to scale profitability is by finding your market's "perfect elasticity point." Here, you'll learn how to run scientific and controlled A/B tests. You'll discover how to test new pricing in international markets, physical products, and corporate consulting without risking your current revenue.

The myth of the perfect conversion (Why selling less can make you earn more)

The biggest analytical mistake in e-commerce and service sales is blindly worshipping the "Conversion Rate." We think that if 10 out of every 100 people buy, we're winning. If we raise the price and now only 7 buy, we panic because the conversion rate has dropped.

But businesses are not sustained by conversion rates; they are sustained by profit margin.

The price testing methodology involves finding that mathematical intersection where the inevitable drop in sales volume is aggressively offset by the increase in net profit margin. If you sell fewer units but operate with a higher margin, you not only maintain (or exceed) your revenue, but you also free up operational bandwidth, reduce logistics costs, and have more budget to bid on keywords in your advertising campaigns.

Let's see how to apply this scientific methodology, isolated and risk-free, in the three major sales ecosystems.

Ecosystem 1: Testing in Digital Publishing and Mass E-Commerce

When you manage a portfolio of over 200 stocks or sell digital tools globally, A/B testing is your most powerful weapon. The international market is the perfect laboratory, because a price that causes friction in one country can be perceived as a bargain in another.

The Geographic Isolation Technique: If your goal is to reach $1,000 in monthly revenue from automated royalties, you can't change the price of your entire catalog at once. You take a specific market as a testing ground.

Imagine you publish an illustrated series like Magical Tales to Dream About or a technical manual for mastering roulette.

1. **Establish the Control Group:**You are maintaining the current price in the United States and Spain.
2. **Isolate the Variable (The Test):**You choose markets with robust economies (France, Italy, Germany, the Netherlands or Australia) and raise the price of your local edition by 20%.
3. **Inject Traffic:**You use your advertising campaigns (Ads) to send consistent traffic for 14 days. Use analytics tools like Helium 10 or Jungle Scout to track how your Best Sales Ranking (BSR) is performing.
4. **Data Reading:**If sales in Germany fall by 5%, but your royalty margin per book rises by 35%, the test is a resounding success. You've just discovered that the German public is price-inelastic. That new figure becomes your standard for Europe.

Ecosystem 2: Testing in Physical and Specialized Niche Products

Testing prices on physical products requires managing inventory and brand perception. You can't show a customer $30 today and $45 tomorrow in the same store without creating distrust.

The "Ghost Packaging" Technique: Suppose you distribute an advanced fermentation formula (like "the bomb") designed to attract large fish, such as cachama, in tournament lakes. You want to know if the market would support a price increase, but you're afraid of scaring off your regular customers.

Instead of raising the price of the base product, you create a Bundle Test:

- You leave your individual formula at the usual price (The Control).
- You launch a variation: The "Tournament Kit". It includes two units of your formula and a small digital user manual, at a price that, mathematically, inflates the cost per unit by 15%.
- **The Result:**You observe where the money is flowing. If serious competitors start snapping up the "Tournament Kit" en masse, the market is telling you they don't care about the price; they care about exclusivity and the complete solution. You've validated that your brand can handle higher prices, paving the way to raise the cost of individual units next fishing season.

Ecosystem 3: Testing in B2B Services and Consulting

In the sale of high-engineering corporate services, there's no algorithm that divides traffic. If you present a proposal for project oversight to supervise an infrastructure project, you can't tell the client, "I'll charge you $10,000, but if you reload the page, it might be $12,000."

The Staggered Cohort Technique is used here.

Imagine you're going to quote on supervising the construction of a road (where your responsibility is to guarantee the precise execution of 9 cm of asphalt, 30 cm of granular base, and 30 cm of crushed stone). You want to raise your fees by 25% because your technical rigor justifies it, but you're afraid of losing contracts.

1. **Protect your current database:**You keep the clients you already have on the old rate (Grandfathering Protocol).
2. **The Test in the "Next in Line":**To the next three new corporate prospects who request a proposal, you present the new rate with the 25% increase. You completely isolate them from your past pricing.
3. **Friction Analysis:**
   o If all three agree without hesitation, your previous price was dangerously low. You've established your new financial floor.
   o If two parties negotiate but agree (using reverse anchoring), the price is correct.
   o If all three reject you outright, arguing that you're out of touch with the market, you haven't lost your business; you've only lost three prospects. For the fourth proposal, adjust the increase to 15% and test again.

The Rule of Pure Data (Beware of hidden variables)

For an A/B test to be statistically valid and not just a guess, you must respect the iron rule of the scientific method: Isolate only one variable at a time.

If you raise the price of a book, change the cover, and also modify the SEO of your metadata all in the same week, and suddenly your sales skyrocket, you won't know what worked. Was it the Halo Effect of the new look, or did the customer perceive more authority because of the higher price? Without knowing, you won't be able to replicate that success across the rest of your catalog (your other 199 books).

If you're going to test the price, freeze absolutely everything else. The same homepage, the same Helium 10 keywords, the same daily advertising spend. Only then will the data you obtain be pure gold.

Tactical Execution Summary

1. **Select your "Guinea Pig":**Don't test with your flagship product ("best seller") if it represents 80% of your revenue, nor with the worst-performing product in your catalog. Choose a product with average performance in a specific international market (e.g., Italy or Australia) to conduct your first price increase experiment this week.

2. **Define your success metric before you begin:**Decide in advance how much of a drop in volume you're willing to tolerate. "If my sales fall by 15% but my net margin rises by 30%, I'll keep the new price." Take the emotion out of the decision.

3. **Use the packaging as radar:**If you have physical inventory, test market elasticity by launching exclusive bundles or kits. It's the quickest way to gauge how much extra money your customers are willing to spend without altering your core offering.

4. **Apply the "Next B2B Customer" rule:**In your next meeting to quote a technical survey or infrastructure supervision, commit to budgeting 20% above your usual rate. The corporate market is designed to absorb inflation for top talent; you just have to dare to ask for it.

Chapter 28: Pricing Mistakes You Can't Afford to Make

The 8 most common traps and how to recognize them before falling into them.

Throughout this manual, we've built a pricing architecture designed to maximize your margins and attract your ideal customer. However, human psychology is fragile under pressure. When sales decline or a corporate client threatens to switch to the competition, panic sets in, and it's easy to sabotage all your hard work. In this chapter, we'll break down eight deadly pitfalls in pricing and presentation. You'll learn to identify these pitfalls in real time so your profitability never again falls victim to your own nerves.

Trap 1: Cost-Plus Pricing

This is the oldest and most destructive financial trap. It involves adding up your operating costs, calculating the value of your working hours, and adding a standard profit margin (for example, 20%).

- **Why it's destroying your business:**It penalizes your expertise. If you're an expert and you do the job in half the time, charging by the hour means you earn less.
- **The symptom:**In a road infrastructure oversight project, you calculate the price based on how many topographical visits you'll make, instead of charging for the monumental risk you're mitigating. The client isn't paying you to "go and look"; they're paying you to ensure that the 9 cm of asphalt, the 30 cm of granular base, and the 30 cm of crushed stone are laid with millimeter tolerances, preventing catastrophic cost overruns. Your price should be a percentage of the disaster you prevent.

Trap 2: The Race to the Bottom (The $0.99 Syndrome)

This happens when you assume that the market is 100% rational and will always choose the cheapest option, leading you to cut your prices to "win by volume".

- **Why it's destroying your business:**Low prices destroy your authority and your operating margins.
- **The symptom:**You publish an advanced manual with mathematical and probability systems for roulette and poker, and price it at $2.99 to compete with generic pamphlets. The professional player, who would truly value your system, sees that price and assumes the content is rubbish for beginners. Furthermore, with such low royalties, trying to sustain Amazon Ads campaigns will leave you in the red after the first click.

Trap 3: Visual dissonance (The Horns Effect)

This trap is triggered when you demand a premium price but the visual ecosystem of your product screams "amateur".

- **Why it's destroying your business:**The human brain does not process intrinsic quality until after the purchase; before the purchase, it only evaluates aesthetics.
- **The symptom:**You package a premium collection of Magical Tales to Dream About, which includes immersive audiobooks generated with advanced AI voice. You price it high, but the listing cover has typos, lacks cinematic lighting, and the description is a dense block of text with no hierarchy. The customer feels an immediate disconnect between what they're asking for and what they're showing, and abandons their cart.

Trap 4: Panic Discounting

It's Friday afternoon, you check your store's sales dashboard and the numbers are frozen. Anxiety spikes and, without any strategy, you slap a 40% discount on your star product hoping to inject some cash.

- **Why it's destroying your business:**You train your client to never pay you the full price.
- **The symptom:**If you sell a highly fermented formula ("the bomb") for sport fishing for cachama and discount it every time there's a tournament coming up, competitors will learn to wait until the week before the event to buy. You've devalued your own technology. Every discount should require something in return (a strict time condition or being tied to a volume purchase).

Trap 5: Geographical Blindness (The Static International Price)

Believing that the value of your product is universal and applying a simple currency conversion when exporting it to new territories.

- **Why it's destroying your business:**It ignores local purchasing power and the perception of cultural value in each region.
- **The symptom:**You launch your digital catalog in the German, French, Italian, and Australian markets using the same pricing structure as in your home country. You're leaving money on the table. A price that seems high in an emerging market might be perceived as suspiciously cheap in Europe or Australia. You need to audit the premium competition in each territory and adjust your prices (for example, to €19.99) to cover the high acquisition costs in those countries.

Trap 6: The Naked Price

This happens when the customer discovers your rate before having internalized the problem you are going to solve for them and the transformation they will experience.

- **Why it's destroying your business:**The price becomes an isolated and painful anchor.
- **The symptom:**Send a B2B proposal where the total cost appears on the first page, or send a PDF where the client can scroll directly to the last line. The price should always be presented in a "sandwich" format: after quantifying the client's financial pain (the cost of not hiring you) and just before detailing the immediate next steps to begin work.

Trap 7: Validate the Comparative Excel

You fall into this trap the moment you agree to discuss with a prospect why your service is more expensive than that of competitor "X" who promises to do the same thing.

- **Why it's destroying your business:**You lower yourself to the category of a generic product (commodity).
- **The symptom:**The client says, "The other agency charges me half." If you respond, "But we're faster and have better support," you've lost. You're justifying operational characteristics. The correct response is to apply Reverse Anchoring: "They operate with a generic volume model. We operate with an absolute risk mitigation model. What is the cost to your company if the cheaper provider makes a mistake?"

Trap 8: Breaking the tactical silence

The most subtle trap, and the one that ruins the most deals at the last second. You reveal your high price and, faced with the client's thoughtful silence, you speak to justify yourself.

- **Why it's destroying your business:**You convey desperation and signal to your buyer's amygdala that your price is a negotiable bluff.
- **The symptom:**"The investment to implement the system is twelve thousand dollars... but, uh, we could review the scope if it goes over budget." You just gave away your profit margin because you couldn't handle ten seconds of tension in the room. State your number with clinical clarity, hold eye contact, and let the client decide their next move.

Preventive Error Audit

To safeguard your operation, review this checklist before sending your next sales quote or publishing a new product in your international catalog:

The Risk	The Control Question
Profitability	Is this price calculated based on the time it will take me, or based on the money I will make the client earn/save?
Positioning	Do the design, cover image, and keywords of my listing visually justify that I am the most expensive option on the site?
Expansion	Have I adjusted this price to the specific purchasing power of the country where my ads are running?
Negotiation	Am I mentally prepared to state the price, keep my mouth shut, and not offer a discount unless the customer gives up part of the product?

Chapter 29: Get Paid What You're Worth: The Final Manifesto

The emotional and rational closure that turns the reader into a professional who never again gives away their work.

We've reached the end of the journey. You've dismantled consumer neuroscience, mastered the Halo Effect, learned to structure risk, and perfected tactical silence. But none of these technical tools will work if your internal financial thermostat is still broken. This chapter isn't a tactic; it's a pact of honor with yourself. It's time to abandon the "budget provider" identity forever and embrace your role as the architect of high-value solutions.

The tragedy of the master's degree in liquidation

Over the years, you've invested countless hours, capital, and vital energy in perfecting your craft. You've learned to read the market, master mathematical probabilities, and structure systems that work.

However, there is a brutal dissonance between what you are capable of delivering and what you dare to charge.

When you lower your price for fear of losing a client, you're not just adjusting a number on an invoice or a digital listing; you're committing an act of self-betrayal. You're telling the market: "All my effort, my technical expertise, and my countless hours of sacrifice are worth less than the temporary peace of mind of not being rejected."

The market is an unforgiving mirror. If you approach it with the energy of someone asking for a favor, you'll be treated as a budget item to be cut. If you charge survival rates, you'll attract clients who demand the world while scrutinizing every penny, stifling your creativity and consuming your free time.

The change of identity: From Operator to Risk Mitigator

True wealth in independent business and strategic publishing doesn't come from working longer hours, but from changing the way you define your own value.

You're not an hourly worker; you're a results protector.

- When you take on the oversight of a major infrastructure project, you're not just getting paid to look at a site. Your signature and your technical expertise don't just approve 9 cm of asphalt, 30 cm of granular base, and 30 cm of crushed stone; your signature is the absolute shield that prevents the project's structural and financial collapse. That certainty is worth its weight in gold.
- When you publish a statistical manual for mastering poker or roulette, you're not selling pages of paper or bytes on a screen. You're selling the mathematical system that will prevent the player from losing their capital at the casino. That tactical advantage is worth its weight in gold.
- When you formulate a specialized, high-fermentation bait, you're not just selling dough in a bag. You're selling the trophy catch (the hefty cachama) from a tournament where the angler has already invested hundreds of dollars. That moment of triumph is worth its weight in gold.

Your premium client doesn't want your time. They want your confidence. They pay high fees because they want to sleep soundly knowing that a true expert is in charge.

The mathematics of scalability demands courage

If your vision is to dominate high-purchasing-power international markets like France, Germany, Italy, the Netherlands, and Australia, financial timidity is your biggest enemy.

You can't scale a catalog to the $1,000 monthly royalty mark if you're charging a dollar margin per sale. You can't dominate bidding in international ad campaigns if your budget doesn't give you the breathing room to crush the competition on cost per click.

Money is simply a tool for measuring energy. By ethically and justifiably raising your prices, you gain the resources to invest in advertising, optimize your SEO, render better homepages, and create ecosystems where low-cost competition simply cannot survive. Charging more is the only viable way to deliver a better product.

The Price Architect's Manifesto

From this moment on, excuses are over. Before you send your next sales proposal or launch your next product, read this manifesto. It's your new non-negotiable reality:

1. **My price is not an apology:**I will never again nervously justify my fee or break the tactical silence. My price is a mathematical reflection of the value of the transformation I deliver.
2. **I'm not competing in the Excel table:**I refuse to participate in the price war. If the client is looking for cuts, I'll show them the door. I operate in the business of risk mitigation and exclusivity, and that doesn't lend itself to generic comparisons.
3. **I embrace friction:**I understand that if no one rejects my prices, it means I'm charging too little. The rejection from unqualified clients isn't a loss; it's a safety net that protects my time for premium clients.
4. **Design visual authority:**My approach will be impeccable. I will never charge high prices while wrapping my product or service in cheap packaging or using mediocre language. My presence will exude authority long before I even mention the price.
5. **My time is sacred:**By increasing my ticket price, I choose to work with less volume and greater impact. I choose profitability over popularity. I choose my own peace of mind over the approval of those who don't value excellence.

You've built the ecosystem. You've shielded yourself from objections. You possess the psychological architecture to make the market reward you exactly as you deserve.

Now, close this book, open your platform, adjust that price tag upwards, and go out and claim the value that has always been yours.

Chapter 30: The Master in Pricing Architecture for Product Ecosystems

The master plan to orchestrate massive catalogs, dominate global niches, and safeguard the value of your physical and digital items.

The modern product creator and seller rarely settles for a single product line. The perfect business ecosystem is multidimensional. You manage global digital publishing empires, develop physical products for hyper-specialized niches, and build collections with high perceived value. Here, we will unify absolutely all the principles in this book into a single "Total Value Ecosystem." You will learn how pricing psychology adapts and feeds back on itself when you operate multiple radically different product lines simultaneously.

The Multidimensional Creator Ecosystem

Throughout this manual, we've broken down tactics for selling without resorting to haggling. True mastery comes when you understand that the Halo Effect, Risk Reversal, and Strategic Packaging are universal principles that allow you to diversify your product catalog without diluting your profitability.

Imagine the architecture of a perfect product ecosystem, divided into three pillars of scalability. This is how pricing psychology is applied at its best to each of them:

Pillar 1: The Global Scalability Vehicle (Digital and Publishing Products)

This pillar is your automated revenue engine. The strategic goal here is to reliably and predictably exceed revenue targets, such as the $1,000 monthly royalty mark, by managing a robust catalog of over 200 titles without relying on algorithmic luck.

- **Price Execution:**Here you apply Geographic Localization and Context Elevation. You don't compete at introductory prices in saturated markets. You position your technical manuals, such as probability systems for mastering poker or roulette, at premium rates in the highest-spending markets (France, Germany, Italy, the Netherlands, and Australia).
- **Status Technology:**To justify these international prices, you inject the visual Halo Effect. You use prompt architecture to generate covers with cinematic lighting and hyper-realistic finishes. You support your listings with hard data extracted from tools like Helium 10 or Jungle Scout to master SEO. By charging a high price, you obtain the exact profit margin to win all bids in advertising campaigns and monopolize the keywords in your niche.

Pillar 2: The Passionate Niche Vehicle (Specialized Physical Products)

The second pillar is the ultimate proof that you understand your consumer's identity and pain points. Here, you master a hyper-segmented physical market where passion clouds the buyer's reasoning.

- **Price Execution:**You don't sell generic components or leisure items; you sell "The Competitive Advantage." If you launch a hyper-fermented bait formula, known as "the bomb," to catch large species like cachama, your product isn't just a commercial mass. It's the exclusive tactical ammunition for ensuring success in tournament lakes.
- **Psychology:**You apply Reverse Anchoring and the Assembly Effect. You take tactical components (high-strength fishing lines, reels imported from Asian platforms) and package them as the Ultimate Tournament Kit. You remind the customer that they've already invested hundreds of dollars in their entry and logistics. Failing by saving a few dollars on bait or hooks is an unacceptable risk. Your product is strategically positioned as the most economical guarantee of

success among the expensive decisions the customer has already made.

Pillar 3: The High-Ticket Hybrid Vehicle (Premium Collections and Bundles)

The third pillar is where you maximize Average Order Value (AOV). Instead of creating dozens of new, low-margin products, you take the assets you already have and merge them into compelling ecosystems that the customer can't compare to anything else on the market.

- **Price Execution:**You use the Three-Tier Architecture. You don't offer individual items that cause decision fatigue.
- **Packaging Technology:**If you have a line of illustrated stories, like the Magical Tales to Dream series, your flagship product will never be a single book. You create a luxury Elite Tier: the complete collection in physical format, accompanied by immersive audiobooks generated using advanced speech synthesis technology. By positioning this high-priced premium option as the anchor, the standard package of your main series automatically becomes the logical, mass-market, and irresistible choice for the buyer.

The Law of Visual Authority Transference

What's fascinating about operating this multidimensional ecosystem of products is that the visual authority you develop in one pillar is transferred to the others.

The analytical rigor you use to structure ad campaigns in Europe, measuring cost per click down to the millimeter, is the same rigor you apply to evaluating the profitability of a new batch of fishing gear. The obsession with cinematic design on a digital cover is the same obsession that will prevent you from packaging a physical product in a generic box.

Your Final Oath as a Product Creator

The digital and physical marketplace is a theater of perceptions. If you present your products competing on the lowest price point, you'll be treated as a disposable brand. If you enter by setting the rules, demonstrating the product's impact, designing impeccable listings, and maintaining your price with absolute firmness against the competition, the market will reward you with profitability.

Review your inventory and dashboard today. Eliminate any discounts that reek of panic. Raise your packaging and metadata standards. Write descriptions that repel novice shoppers and attract customers willing to invest.

You have the three-tier structure, the prompt architecture to master the visuals, and the data intelligence to conquer multiple international markets. The ecosystem is complete. Now, update those price tags and go out and claim the true value of what you've created.

Dear reader,

First and foremost, I want to thank you for taking the time to explore the pages of "Neuromarketing: The Value of Price. Psychological Keys to Setting Successful Prices." This book has been an exciting journey, and it has been written with the purpose of providing valuable tools and knowledge that you can apply in your professional and personal life.

Each chapter has been carefully crafted to give you a deep understanding of how price can influence consumer decisions and how you can use these strategies to create value and success. I sincerely hope that this book inspires you and gives you new perspectives on approaching neuromarketing.

If you have found value and resonance in these pages, I would be very happy if you would share your thoughts and experiences. Your words will not only help me continue to improve, but they could also guide and motivate others who seek to better understand neuromarketing.

With gratitude and appreciation,
Jimmy Fajardo